In Search of Truth

In
Search
of
Truth

Three Yeshiva Students
on a Spiritual Journey

MENACHEM BROD

In Search of Truth
First English Edition – Tishrei 5783 / October 2022

Translated from the Hebrew נשמה עם עצמה
Neshama Im Atzma (The Soul Alone)

Menachem Brod
PO Box 327
Kfar Chabad, Israel 6084000
972-3-960-6628
brod-m@chabad.org.il

Translated by: Shprintza Goldberg
Edited by: Daniel Goldberg
Typeset by: Yoel Broderick
sefarim.in.design@gmail.com

Distributed by:
BSD Publishers
347-560-9770
info@BSDpublishers.com
www.BSDpublishers.com

Printed in China
ISBN: 978-1-945288-96-8

CONTENTS

PREFACE

This book was originally published in Hebrew in 5764 (2004) under the title *Neshama Im Atzma*. Its chapters had first appeared in weekly installments in the Hebrew-language *Kfar Chabad* magazine during the years 1984-1985, and they captivated the readers. Many suggested that they be published in book form. Meanwhile, others already collected copies of the installments and distributed them to those interested.

After its publication as a book, it became a best-seller among both youth and adults, yeshiva students and high school and seminary girls, from Chassidic and non-Chassidic backgrounds, orthodox and modern-orthodox and even those not yet Torah-observant. For them all, this book opened a window into the inner world of Chabad Chassidism.

Over the years since, I have received many enthusiastic comments from readers. Many declared that the book has changed their lives. Its form as a novel allowed readers to relate more authentically to its themes, and its heroes' inner struggles touched readers' hearts, enabling them to identify with its characters' experiences.

One reader who had become a *baal teshuva* (returnee to Judaism) many years ago told me, "After finishing the book I realized I had to do my *teshuva* all over again!" A Chassidic father told me, "When I brought the book home, my daughter, a high school student, grabbed it and read through the whole book almost in a single sitting. She told me it had taught her so many new ideas, and above all what *Chassidus* is all about." A Chabad *shaliach* gave the book to a member of an Israeli *kibbutz* he had met. A few days later, the man told him, "I've been all over the world, yet only in this book have I found G-d! It has given me answers to very many questions that have bothered me."

I am especially grateful to my son, Shmuel Gershon Halevi, who, while still in yeshiva, regularly urged me to take time from my many urgent pursuits to prepare the installments for publication as a book. Thanks also to my son, Shneur Zalman Halevi, who helped ensure accuracy of the Hebrew text and gave good advice.

Thank you, Rabbi Aharon Dov Halperin, editor of *Kfar Chabad* magazine, for your original initiative to write this story and for your assistance while I was writing it, and thank you also for writing your enthusiastic foreword to the book, which is translated here.

I express my deep gratitude to the many wonderful Jews who helped me originally to write the series in the *Kfar Chabad*, by describing in detail their personal stories and inner struggles that accompanied their search for "the inner light of the Torah." Because so many years have passed since then, I am not sure I remember all their names, so I will suffice with a general expression of gratitude to them all.

My deepest thanks to Mrs. Shprintza Goldberg of Toronto, Canada, who told me how profoundly impressed she was by the book to the extent that she volunteered to translate it into English in order to make it accessible to the vast English-speaking readership. Thanks also to Reb Daniel Goldberg of

Crown Heights, New York (the two Goldbergs are not related), for his attentive editing of the translation and for carefully adapting the content, in several places, for an English-speaking audience.

I pray that this translation of my book be positively received by the public, and may it arouse readers' hearts to serve G-d with true vitality and with a sense of "Taste and see that *Hashem* is good." May we be privileged very soon to experience revelation of the true Divine light in all its glory, in the true and complete *Geula* (Redemption) by our righteous *Moshiach*.

Menachem Mendel Halevi Brod
Kfar Chabad, the Holy Land
Summer, 5782 (2022)

FOREWORD

(To the first Hebrew edition of *Neshama Im Atzma*)
By Aharon Dov Halperin, Editor of *Kfar Chabad* magazine

This book brings back pleasant memories of the early years of the *Kfar Chabad* magazine, after we celebrated its 100th issue. Along with our gratification at what it had accomplished and how wonderfully it had developed, we still sought ways to express more powerfully the remarkable spiritual treasures concealed within the world of *Chassidus*.

My own personal journey had intensified my awareness of this deficiency. Despite being born into a Chabad family, I had spent my youth studying in non-Chassidic Torah schools, so that the inner light of *Chassidus* had remained beyond me.

Only a long, challenging process enabled me to discover the exalted illumination of *Chassidus*. Many fellow yeshiva students from a variety of backgrounds experienced the same process, as they too became attracted to its bright light.

It all began at extra-curricular classes we attended to study *Tanya*, the fundamental text of *Chassidus*, authored by the Alter Rebbe (1745-1812), the founder of Chabad. Gradually it exposed us to the limitless spiritual wealth of *Chassidus*. Those classes convinced me, among many others, to adopt the path of *Chassidus* as our own. Some participants in those classes may not have actually become Chassidim but are still forever grateful to those who opened their eyes to the boundless spiritual depth of Chabad.

When the *Kfar Chabad* Magazine was launched, one of its principal goals was to bring the light of *Chassidus* to the broader public outside Chabad's inner circle. Nevertheless, after the magazine's 100th issue, I felt we still had not yet succeeded in imparting that special sense of "Taste and see that *Hashem* is good" (as the Alter Rebbe once expressed it) – of how deeply stimulating and inspiring is the deep understanding of the Divine attained by studying *Chassidus*.

True, *Kfar Chabad* had published dozens of the Rebbe's brilliant Torah discussions (*sichos*), and many profound essays of Torah thought by outstanding Chabad mentors. We had publicized moving narratives of Chassidic history and inspiring articles, and had described in detail the awesome achievements – unprecedented in Jewish history – of the Rebbe's emissaries in spreading authentic Jewish values, especially as illuminated by the teachings of *Chassidus*, to Jews around the world. We had worked to impart a sense of the Rebbe's great light and the powerful spiritual experience of time spent close to him, in prayer, at his *farbrengens* (great Chassidic public gatherings), and in private meetings with him (*yechidus*).

Still, despite all our efforts, I still felt that the illuminating, uplifted feeling flooding through me when first exposed to *Chassidus* had not yet been well expressed. Not only was this urgently needed for the wider circle of readers, but even for those born and raised within Chabad-Lubavitch. Often I sensed that many members of our own community do not always fully appreciate the spiritual wealth with which they live. Concepts that for me were illuminating and eye-opening are so often taken for granted and their significance not fully recognized.

Rabbi Menachem (Mendy) Brod, a gifted young man then at the start of his literary career, had just begun to write regularly for *Kfar Chabad* magazine. As I observed and was impressed by his unusual talents, I shared with him my above thoughts. His rare combination of deep understanding and clear writing convinced me he would be capable of accomplishing this daunting task in an exemplary way.

I began to relate to him the long process I had experienced, along with many fellow yeshiva students, in those *Tanya* classes – the doubts and hesitations each had felt on one hand, and the sense of wonderment and sweetness from the bright light bursting into our souls on the other. I referred him to other young men whose experiences had paralleled mine, and he avidly listened to their personal stories. Based on all this, he started the amazing serial, "*Neshama Im Atzma*" ("The Soul with Itself"), which captured our readers' hearts from its first chapter.

Some have tried to find similarities between the story's characters and specific individuals. But that is pointless, because this is not a factual story about any real person but a work of total fiction. Nevertheless, as we saw Mendy Brod's narrative unfold, I and many of my friends felt it accurately described our own spiritual experiences and accompanying feelings. From that perspective, the book is fully true to life.

The many years since this story's original publication have not diminished its beauty at all. Even today, it is captivating and inspiring, shining bright light on the inner spiritual world of *Chassidus*. Perhaps, if written today, it would need to address other issues, too. Nevertheless, I believe the author did well to republish the story in its original form and unique flavor.

This book will bring blessed illumination to every Jew who seeks spiritual truth. It should be mandatory reading even for every member of the Chabad community, especially for youth and yeshiva students who, like this story's characters, are often troubled by similar questions and doubts. Reading this book will give them a taste of the source of Torah light revealed by our Rebbes in Chabad *Chassidus*.

Publishing this series as a book is another step in fulfilling the goal set before the Baal Shem Tov (1698-1760), the founder of the Chassidic movement, when he experienced his renowned "ascent of the soul" to the heavenly abode of the soul of *Moshiach*. The Baal Shem Tov asked him, "When will you arrive?" And *Moshiach* replied, "When the wellsprings of your teachings will spread outwards" – when *Chassidus* will be spread out to the furthest reaches of the Jewish world. May we be privileged that this goal be realized very soon, with the revelation of our righteous *Moshiach*!

In Search of Truth

CHAPTER ONE
A THOUGHT-PROVOKING BUS-RIDE

Just moments before, the yeshiva's great hall had been full with dozens of young men sitting over their *Gemaras* (volumes of Talmud). But now it slowly emptied. The hum of study echoing through the *beis hamidrash* gradually ceased as the late hour sent the students one by one to their bedrooms. Just a few students remained, those who usually sat up late on Thursday nights to continue studying. Scattered around the hall, they were still fully absorbed in study.

Aharon loved these hours in the stillness of the night, when the study hall emptied out and silence reigned. More than any other time, he enjoyed these late night hours, fully identifying with our Sages' statement that "The night was created only for Torah study." These were his best hours which he awaited all week long, when he could let himself forgo his sleep and immerse himself entirely in Torah study.

Sometimes, when his classmates seemed in no hurry to go, Aharon would silently wish for them to leave soon. After wishing for this, however, he would always berate himself for preferring his own peace and quiet to the Torah study of so many fellow students. Nevertheless, it was as if they heard his plea, for soon, one by one, they would begin to close their *Gemaras*, and within a short time Aharon would be alone in his corner. And then his special hours would finally start.

This evening, however, other thoughts were distracting him.

Never before did Aharon have trouble focusing during this special time. Yet now he simply couldn't concentrate. As long as the sound of Torah study had echoed through the study hall, he had been able to immerse himself in study. But now, in the almost unbroken silence, Aharon began to feel that his thoughts were elsewhere. He tried to overcome this by redirecting his focus to the page he was studying. But before long he was staring out into space again, his thoughts far away.

An uncomfortable feeling took hold of him, a sense of suffocation. No longer could he stay at his place in the *beis hamidrash*, as a deep impulse pushed him to escape into the fresh air and the open space beyond. Abruptly he stood up, closed his *Gemara*, and left the *beis hamidrash*.

To bring some order to his thoughts, he needed time alone. The cool night air striking his face froze him momentarily in his tracks. Breathing in the clear air that filled his lungs calmed him a little, and a sense of relief passed through him. But his mental confusion did not subside. He sought a private place where he could sit alone with his thoughts.

His legs brought him to the field behind the yeshiva. He continued walking until he came upon a large rock under an ancient olive tree, from where the yeshiva buildings seemed so distant.

"That's it!" he cried out as he sat down. "I must decide, right now, which direction to take!"

* * *

Aharon's thoughts took him back to a bus ride he had taken to Yerushalayim about two years ago. He remembered the kindly-looking young man who sat down next to him, and recalled his surprise at the man's simple greeting to a total stranger:

"Hi! If *Hashem* has arranged for us to sit next to each other, it must be for some purpose. But if we just sit quietly through our whole ride, it'll be as if we've never met. On the other hand, if we have a conversation, maybe we'll both get some benefit from it."

Aharon was not used to speaking to strangers. In fact, he didn't like speaking much at all. When he rode a bus, he preferred reading a book or just watching the landscape and allowing his thoughts to wander freely. But this pleasant young man next to him grabbed his attention, and he responded positively.

The young man's name was Shmuel. Even before he mentioned his land of origin, his accent betrayed his background from the Soviet Union. He had emigrated from there, he said, just three years earlier. Learning this drew Aharon closer to him because, without knowing exactly why, he had always admired the fascinating secret life of Jews behind the Iron Curtain.

A year before the family left for Israel, Shmuel related, his father had passed away from a severe illness. Often, he continued, he missed the late nights spent alone with his father, sitting in a concealed room to study Torah together. That study had been something special, with every line they studied, every concept they grasped, infusing them with renewed vitality. That Torah study was so alive and revitalizing, like cool water refreshing someone's thirst.

"What did you study then?" Aharon asked.

"We would learn *Chumash* with Rashi's commentary, *Mishna, Gemara*, and some *Tanya*," Shmuel replied.

The word "*Tanya*" rang a bell in Aharon's mind. "He must be a Chabad *Chassid*," he thought, making a mental note to himself. It aroused his curiosity. He had heard much about Chassidim, but at that time had never actually spoken to one.

"You had a connection to Chabad?" he asked.

"Yes," replied Shmuel. "My grandfather was a *Chassid* of the Rebbe RaShaB, Rabbi Sholom Ber of Lubavitch, and he had studied in that Rebbe's famous *Yeshivas Tom'chei T'mimim* there. My father would often say that the only way our family succeeded in remaining faithful to the Torah under the Communist regime was thanks to *Tanya*."

This seemed a great opportunity for Aharon to probe further into the subject of Chassidim and *Chassidus*. Meanwhile, he referred to their previous subject of conversation.

"You don't need to miss the Torah study you had back in Russia, which must have been minimal and limited," Aharon said. "*Boruch Hashem*, we have many yeshivos here in the Holy Land where students study Torah in depth, and you can feel fortunate you've been able to immigrate and study here."

"Of course," Shmuel clarified. "I'm overjoyed to be in the Land of our Forefathers, which has so many special qualities. On the other hand, I feel something is missing here. It's difficult to articulate, but something seems to be lacking."

"I suppose you're referring to the prevailing secular culture," Aharon suggested, trying to understand. "But aren't you impressed by all the yeshivos here, and the amazing growth of Torah education, with so many thousands of young people studying Torah full time."

"Of course," Shmuel agreed. "That's all wonderful. But I'll tell you the truth: Sometimes I don't understand why many of them are studying Torah in general."

"What?" Aharon reacted sharply, as if stung by a snake. "What do you mean, 'Why are they studying?' What then should they be doing?"

"You know what?" Shmuel challenged him, "Let's not talk about others. Let's start with you. You study in a yeshiva. Why are you studying?"

"How can you ask that?" said Aharon, starting to get annoyed. "We're trying to become Torah scholars, and it's impossible to to do that without studying. What is there not to understand?"

"Please don't get worked up," said Shmuel in a soothing voice. "Let's talk calmly. But just listen to what you said. You study Torah in order to be a Torah scholar. And what is a Torah scholar? Someone who studies Torah. So we have a circular argument: You're studying because you're a Torah scholar, and why are you a Torah scholar? Because you study. But the essential question is: Why do you want to be a Torah scholar? Why do you study?"

Aharon recalled now what he had once heard in yeshiva about Chassidim, that some scorned Torah study. At the time, he had dismissed such reports, for surely Chassidim have so many yeshivos where thousands of students study Torah. But now he began to suspect that maybe those rumors had some basis. He decided to explore this further and discover whether it had any truth.

"So what are you saying?" Aharon responded, in an irritated tone. "That there's no need to study Torah? Shouldn't a Jewish youth's world be focused entirely on Torah? What then should we do?"

"Why are you getting so excited?" Shmuel asked. "I never implied anything nor came to any conclusions. I just want to clarify with you this subject that often bothers me. So, I ask you again, and please, don't get sidetracked, but just try to answer my question: Why indeed should we study Torah? In order to properly fulfill all *mitzvos* of the Torah, we can study the *Shulchan Aruch* thoroughly, becoming expert in all Torah laws. What's the purpose of investing so much effort in delving our minds into subjects that often, even usually, have no practical relevance?"

Aharon began to feel uncomfortable. "Well, the Torah sharpens our minds. When we learn *Gemara* with commentaries of the *Rishonim* and the *Acharonim*, our mind becomes much sharper, and we're able to understand everything much more easily."

Shmuel glared at him, until Aharon became embarrassed.

"For that we learn Torah," Shmuel rebuked, "to sharpen our intellect? So the Torah is just a tool to achieve better brain power? Maybe we should play chess or solve crossword puzzles, for they too sharpen our minds. Or maybe the difference is that the Torah is a better mind sharpener?"

"Okay, I agree that what I said doesn't make much sense," Aharon admitted. But he recalled that that's what his yeshiva teacher had told him when he wanted to motivate him to study more. But probably he told him that because he knew it would indeed motivate him.

"So, what's the real reason why we study Torah?" Shmuel persisted.

Aharon was perplexed. "I'll tell you the truth," he said. "I never thought I needed to find a reason to study Torah. It's our way of life. It's what differentiates us from people in the street, as the *Gemara* quotes Rav Yosef who would make a feast every year in honor of *Shavuos*, the day the Torah was given. He would say, 'If not for this day, I would be like any other Yosef in the street.' It's just self-understood that we need to study!"

"Well, for me it's not self-understood," Shmuel retorted. "And I'll tell you something else: Now it's much clearer to me what's missing here. Missing is that connection with the Torah that we had in Russia."

"To what are you referring?" Aharon asked.

"I'll tell you exactly what I mean," said Shmuel. "We've been discussing now for half an hour why we need to study Torah, and not even once have I heard from you the word '*Hashem*.' In Russia, it was obvious that we were studying Torah to become united with *Hashem*, to become connected with His G-dliness. That's why we studied the Torah, and we felt that during those precious moments when we studied it there. But here this feeling seems to be missing."

"Okay, obviously that's the general goal of all Torah and *mitzvos*!" Aharon agreed. "That's why we keep *mitzvos* and why we're careful not to transgress. It's all to fulfill *Hashem*'s will."

"Okay," said Shmuel, "but it didn't occur to you even once to say that in reply to my question."

Aharon fell silent, ashamed of himself. It felt very unpleasant, but Shmuel's sincerity and the truth he radiated compelled Aharon to respond in kind.

"You're right," he said, turning to Shmuel. "This awareness really is missing among us. But maybe it's just natural that, in the Land of Israel, where there's no need for us to demonstrate self-sacrifice for our Jewishness at every step, this awareness has weakened. But when you were in Russia, you felt that Torah study was your victory over the atheistic regime, that it was your connection to your Jewish identity and to *Hashem*. But here we find it harder to feel that."

"I'm not blaming anyone or trying to fault you," Shmuel replied softly. "It could certainly be that here, in Israel, much more effort is needed to come to feel this. But the fact remains that that is the actual situation, and you agree with me that it's not desirable."

Shmuel fell into silence, musing. Aharon stared out of his bus window at the hills surrounding Yerushalayim and contemplated the matter.

He recalled how a *baal teshuva* (returnee to Torah observance) had joined his yeshiva and used to sit not far from him in the study hall. Aharon loved watching him as he studied, for his eyes seemed to shine with an exalted light, his face glowed, and his whole being radiated holiness.

That *baal teshuva*'s image stood now in Aharon's mind. He had always been careful to wash his hands properly before he studied Torah, and he would approach *Gemara* study with respect and awe. His enthusiasm did not come from any brilliant flash of understanding or from the profundity of the concepts studied. It was a holy exhilaration. Aharon had envied him.

Once, Aharon had a discussion with him. The *baal teshuva* expressed shock that some students could laugh freely in the middle of studying Torah. "How can they do that?" he wondered. "Don't our Sages say that when a Jew studies Torah, *Hashem* studies opposite him?"

Aharon had smiled to hear that student's innocent simplicity. Deep in his heart, though, he too wished to have such wholesome sincerity. At the time, it had seemed strange and out of place. But now Aharon was upset with himself why he had not felt it important to learn from him.

Shmuel interrupted Aharon's thoughts. "It seems to me that this problem is evident in observance of *mitzvos*, too. More and more, I get the impression that people keep *mitzvos* only out of habit. They put on *tefilin* because they did it yesterday and the day before. They just don't feel the G-dly aspect of it."

"That's true to some extent," Aharon conceded. "But during prayer and observance of *mitzvos*, it seems to be easier to feel a connection to *Hashem* than while studying *Gemara* about, for instance, 'an ox that gored a cow.' Try to feel a connection with

Hashem when you're discussing what payment is necessary for the damages of an ox goring a cow!"

"When you're talking about our feelings," answered Shmuel, "perhaps you're right. The fact is, though, that the union with *Hashem* that happens when you study Torah and what it says about an ox goring a cow, is infinitely greater than the union with *Hashem* that happens by just putting on *tefilin*, for example."

"How can that be?" Aharon asked, puzzled.

Instead of answering directly, Shmuel took a little book out of his pocket. "First read what's written here in *Tanya*," he told Aharon.

It was the first time Aharon had ever held a *Tanya* in his hands. Shmuel had opened it to Chapter 4, pointing to words explaining that the Torah and its *mitzvos* are, so to speak, united with *Hashem*'s Essence. It quoted the *Zohar* (the main work of mystical Torah teaching known as the *Kabbala*) which states that "The Torah and *Hashem* are one." The RaMBaM, too, in his great code of Torah law, states, "He [*Hashem*] is the one who Knows and He is the Knowledge, etc."

"Okay. But where do we see that the Torah is greater than *mitzvos*?" asked Aharon. "It states here that *mitzvos*, too, are united with *Hashem*."

"To understand that, continue to Chapter 5." Shmuel told him.

Intrigued, Aharon proceeded to the next chapter:

"This *halacha* [Torah law] is *Hashem*'s Wisdom and Will: That it has arisen in His Will that when 'Reuven' will argue thus, for example, and 'Shimon' [will counter] thus, then the ruling between them shall be thus. Even if this case never happened and never will happen to come to court on these arguments and claims, nevertheless, since it has so arisen in *Hashem*'s Will and Wisdom that if one will argue thus and the other thus, the ruling shall be thus, [therefore] when a person knows and grasps with his intellect this *halacha* as set forth in the *Mishna* or *Gemara* or [later] Halachic authorities, then he grasps and understands and encompasses with his mind *Hashem*'s Will and Wisdom, [although, otherwise] 'no thought can grasp Him,' nor His Will or His Wisdom..."

"What is this telling us?" asked Aharon.

"Wait a moment," replied Shmuel. "Continue to read another two lines."

"[This] is an amazing union to which no other union can be compared, for there is no other union at all like it or comparable to it in the physical realm, to be one and united literally from every side and angle."

"What does that mean?" Aharon asked.

"It's quite clear really," Shmuel explained. "When you put on *tefilin*, for example, three separate entities are converging together – you, the *tefilin*, and *Hashem* who commanded you to put them on. But although all three converge in that act, they do not become united as one. You still remain separate from the *tefilin*, and you don't feel how you become one with *Hashem*.

"Torah study is different. You, the Torah you study, and

Hashem, who gave the Torah, all become one entity in your mind. When the mind understands a Torah concept, which is *Hashem*'s Wisdom and Will, then the Torah is in your mind, and it becomes united with *Hashem*, too, who is the source of the Torah. You can't separate them. The understanding you have in your mind is the Torah, which is one with *Hashem*. That's why the union achieved through Torah study is so much greater."

"That's very interesting," Aharon mused. "But I'm not sure that people like us, who study in yeshiva and have not yet mastered the entire Talmud with its commentaries and all Halachic authorities, are able to understand and feel such concepts, which really are relevant only to *tzaddikim* who are on a high spiritual level."

"On the contrary," Shmuel disagreed, "this awareness is accessible to every single Jew, not just *tzaddikim*."

"So why do we find this only in *Chassidus*, which are works of Torah secrets," asked Aharon triumphantly, "and not in Torah sources studied by everyone?"

Shmuel smiled. "There's nothing in *Chassidus* that can't be found in *Nigleh*, in the works of 'revealed' Torah studied by everyone."

Aharon raised his eyebrows.

Shmuel's eyes sparkled mischievously. Opening his briefcase, he took out a *Gemara*. It was *maseches* (tractate) *Kiddushin*. "This is what I'm studying now," he explained.

In his mind, Aharon flew through the pages of *Kiddushin*,

which he had studied last year and committed to memory in its entirety, trying to guess which passage Shmuel had in mind to prove his point.

To Aharon's surprise, however, Shmuel just opened the book's cover and passed him a worn photocopied page he kept there. "This is a copy of a passage from the *BaCh* – the *Bayis Chodosh*, by Rabbi Yoel Sirkes, one of the main commentaries on the *Tur*, the renowned Halachic code authored by one of the greatest *Rishonim*. It's in *Orach Chayim*, Chapter 47, which deals with laws of Torah study. The *BaCh* explains the inner intent a Jew should have when he studies Torah."

Aharon started to read:

> "We should study the Torah in order to unite our soul with the Essence and spirituality and holiness of the Source from where the Torah derives... If people would study the Torah with this intent, they would become a vehicle and chamber for *Hashem*'s Divine presence, which would literally dwell within them, because they are *Hashem*'s chamber, and literally within them the Divine presence has established its dwelling."

"You see," said Shmuel, "this exact concept is written explicitly in a book of *Halacha* that applies to everyone. Since I was shown these words of the *BaCh*, I read them every time before I start to learn Torah."

Aharon was dumbstruck. He had not expected such a clear, irrefutable proof. He thought a little about the words he had just read, and commented, "The problem is really how to feel this."

"When a person studies *Chassidus*, he can come to feel this too," Shmuel replied.

The bus pulled into Yerushalayim's central bus station and came to a stop, ending their conversation. Shmuel bid farewell to Aharon, expressing the hope to meet again sometime. Aharon responded likewise, really hoping they **could** meet again, though he didn't have the courage to ask Shmuel for his address.

Deep in thought, Aharon got off the bus and walked slowly to the next bus that would take him to his destination. This conversation had shifted something deep within him, but what exactly it was, Aharon would find out only some time later.

CHAPTER TWO
TWO COMPANIONS

Aharon studied at a yeshiva for young teenaged boys, which in Israel is called "*yeshiva ketana*" (junior yeshiva), and in America *mesivta* (yeshiva high school). Presently he was in *shiur gimmel*, the third and highest level. His class was large and very lively. Most of his classmates were highly gifted, probably including some of the best yeshiva students in the Holy Land. It was an exemplary class and the yeshiva administration was proud of it.

Among all these special students Aharon was exceptional. His classmates admired him, appreciating his straightforwardness and generous character. They respected his brilliant mind, and how he delved into every detail. When Aharon asked a question, even the *Mashgiach* (dean of students) and the Talmud lecturers knew they had to think hard before answering. They loved debating with him in study for they knew he gave deep, serious thought to his every word and any interaction with him would be a stimulating challenge.

Aharon stood out also because of the quiet, calm energy he exuded. Never did he lose control of himself, nor could his classmates even imagine him getting worked up about anything. He remained cool, calm and collected in every situation. Classmates called him "the class brain," for he was always the most logical and level-headed of them all, and nothing important was decided in the class without him.

His manner of speech, too, was calm, moderate and controlled, even during the most heated debates. A certain quality of his seemed to compel everyone to listen to him, even when he spoke quietly. He didn't need to raise his voice to command attention. Often, especially at the dining room table, stormy arguments broke out among students. Aharon would listen quietly to what everyone said, and only after understanding every participant's position would he quietly and confidently express his opinion. Everyone else would fall silent as they listened to his measured words, and usually most would agree he was right.

Aharon's *chavrusa* (study partner) was his complete opposite. Bentzion was a lively boy, vivacious and full of energy, like a compressed spring waiting to be released at any moment. If he needed to consult some *sefer* (Torah book) during one of the study sessions, he wouldn't walk over to the bookshelf but would almost run there in his unique jumpy way.

Bentzion's train of thought was like that, too. He didn't think much before he spoke, nor did he examine in depth what he was about to say. His questions and answers were hasty, impulsive reactions, and sometimes even he himself would burst out laughing on realizing the implication of what had tumbled out of his mouth. But his classmates loved him for his bright energy and the liveliness and joy of life that characterized his every step.

Yet Bentzion was not shallow. Blessed with a sharp mind and quick grasp, his impulsiveness masked his sharpness and depth. Those unfamiliar with him may have had the impression that he was flippant and superficial, but it was misleading. Whoever spent more time with him soon discovered his special qualities. Despite his cheery and energetic personality, deep within Bentzion was profoundly serious.

Initially, when Aharon and Bentzion first became close friends and began to study together, it was the talk of the yeshiva. A companionship between such two opposites seemed unimaginable. But what appeared so strange at first seemed perfect as time passed. Their study partnership was a great success, and together the two advanced amazingly in their studies.

Aharon had initiated this strange friendship. Perhaps he was the only one capable of truly appreciating Bentzion's rich inner world, to notice the deep sensitivity concealed beneath his mask of high spirits and playfulness. And Aharon needed that. Sensing that he would find in Bentzion the companion he sought, his instincts indeed did not mislead him.

What originally brought them together was an incident in the yeshiva dining room. On a rainy winter day, when the wind howled outside and stormy rain struck the windows noisily, the students sat down to eat their warm lunch. Just then, an elderly, hunched-over man appeared in the dining room doorway. He had an unkempt beard, his clothing was tattered, and water dripped from his clothes and hat. As he stood there watching the boys satisfy their hunger, he obviously was hoping someone would approach him.

But no one paid him any attention. With a deep sigh, he walked with heavy steps to an empty chair next to a vacant table and sat down, resting his head on his hands.

As the old man's dark eyes, full of acute pain, looked around apathetically, Aharon could easily discern the deep lines on his long thin face. He had a troubled expression that bespoke profound suffering. It was clear he had endured much in his life. Yet he seemed different from the other homeless people who hung out in the streets. His face had a certain refined quality, and his suffering eyes had a look of wisdom born of life experience.

Like the other students, Aharon generally avoided such people, disliking their company. Their neglected appearance, usually filthy, and the great suffering that seemed to burst forth from them, engendered a feeling of disgust even in a sensitive boy like Aharon. This vagrant guest would have sat there until the meal was over, with no one approaching to ask what he needed.

As their meal was coming to its end, however, Elimelech entered the dining room. He was always the last to get his meal. Fellow students thought that his consistent late-coming expressed a desire to avoid the meal's excitement and the heated conversations around the table during and after eating. Elimelech, it seemed, preferred to eat alone, in solitude and silence.

In general, Elimelech seemed somewhat odd. He obviously liked to be alone. When conversations and debates broke out in the classroom, he did not participate. In his studies, though, he was an outstanding student, among the best in the class, and was considered its biggest *masmid*, the most diligent and assiduous class member. But his distance from the class's social life placed his talents in the shadows. To his fellow students, Elimelech existed yet also didn't exist, so to speak, at one and the same time.

Some recalled that Elimelech had not always been that way. Originally, they said, he had been a playful boy full of energy, who did not naturally remain alone in his own corner. No one knew what had caused the sudden radical change in Elimelech. But no one really paid much attention. His present conduct now merged so seamlessly into his new persona that before long everyone thought of it as part of his essential character.

At night, after the official study sessions were over, Elimelech would sit in a corner of the yeshiva's library room, engrossed in various rare Torah works, usually small-format books, some of them so old that they were crumbling. No one knew what he studied there, because no one ever bothered asking. It seemed self-understood that Elimelech, the odd student, was involved in studying odd subjects. Even his roommates who may have noticed him coming to bed late at night accepted his conduct as perfectly natural.

On this stormy day, as Elimelech entered the dining room, his sharp eyes locked onto the lonely man sitting by the empty table. Immediately he grasped the situation. Quietly and unobtrusively, he took his plate of food and set it in front of the old man.

"Here, this is for you," he told him.

Elimelech went to wash his hands for bread and sufficed with just a few slices of bread and some fruits left on the table.

Most students didn't notice what Elimelech had done so quietly. Chattering and laughing, they left the hall in groups, giving no more thought to the old tramp who was now gulping down his meal hungrily.

But Aharon's table was close by, and those sitting there were among the few to notice. At first, they didn't bother relating to it. After all, it was Elimelech who had done it, and Elimelech was known to be odd. But soon they started to comment.

"If he wants to stay hungry, let him stay hungry!" said one.

"Now this man will show up here every day," said another. "And Elimelech will surely share his meal with him, like clockwork."

"For all I care, let him feed and support all the beggars," said a third.

"Wait, isn't there a Halachic concern here about stealing? Did the contributors to the yeshiva donate their money for these beggars to eat here?"

"No, that doesn't matter. Elimelech gave up his meal to that man. He's allowed to do that."

"But surely, if Elimelech doesn't want to eat, he should return his portion to the yeshiva. He has no right to give it away to strangers."

"But there's another Halachic issue here, of *bittul Torah* – wasting Torah study. Without eating properly, how will he be able to concentrate on his studies? A yeshiva student has no permission to give up his meal. If he's still hungry, he'll lose proper concentration on his Torah learning!"

"Someone should chase out these people before they even come in. Is this a soup kitchen?"

Aharon sat listening to the flow of comments and arguments. What he heard filled him with disgust. Perhaps, he thought, if the yeshiva were overrun by such people, there might be some reason for debating whether they should be given to eat. But if it happens so rarely that a hungry Jew appears, and someone decides to give up his meal for him, should that student be treated with contempt? Surely this is the highest way to fulfill the *mitzva* of *tzedaka* (charity).

The argument among the students became very heated. Occasionally, they erupted in laughter with jibes at Elimelech's expense.

Suddenly, Aharon noticed that Bentzion, too, was sitting there brooding like him. Although usually he was an active participant in every discussion and debate, this time he did not join in. He sat at the end of the table, deep in thought, staring at the stormy rain pelting the windows.

A joke and a great burst of laughter brought the discussion to a close. The boys recited *birkas hamazon* (the blessings after meals of bread) and left the dining hall. Only Aharon and Bentzion stayed at the table, as if by some silent agreement.

Aharon was surprised to see how Bentzion's blue eyes, which were usually dancing, had a faraway look. His face, usually bright with energy, was now serious. At that moment, Aharon perceived another facet of Bentzion's personality, one of deep feeling and sensitivity.

A few moments later, Bentzion shook himself from his thoughts. Except for Bentzion and Aharon, only the elderly visitor was still in the dining room, scraping the last morsels from his plate, and Elimelech, sitting at the other end of the room, slowly eating his slice of bread.

"Did you hear their argument?" Bentzion asked Aharon.

"Yes, and it was not pleasant to hear," Aharon replied.

"You know," Bentzion said, "Their apathy was shocking. From where do we get this indifference? A hungry Jew comes into the dining room, and not a single person thinks to give him even a piece of bread, except Elimelech..."

"Most perplexing," observed Aharon, "was how they were so involved in their debates, in questions of theft and *bittul Torah*... The man could have died of hunger while they were still busy with their debates!"

"Did you see how hungrily the poor man gulped down his food?" said Bentzion. "He must have been starved."

"Yes," Aharon responded scornfully, "but, according to our fellow students, there seems to be a question of *bittul Torah*..."

"That's what was so ridiculous about it," Bentzion said. "You understand, to give up a meal just once for a hungry Jew is *bittul Torah*, and to see a hungry man watching longingly while all the boys are eating, that's keeping Torah?"

"There's a story," Aharon observed, "about someone who brought his son to a famous *Rov*, and told him proudly that his son had learned by heart the entire *maseches Bava Basra*, the longest in the whole Talmud. The *Rov* looked at the boy, whose modish clothing and hairstyle did not reflect those of a serious yeshiva student and asked, 'He may have learned the whole *masechta*, but what did the *masechta* teach **him**?'

"You know," commented Aharon, "we see from here that the

Torah has taught Elimelech something. The question is what has it taught those students so concerned about *bittul Torah*?"

"What a strange, interesting boy Elimelech is," Bentzion said, as he watched him.

Just then Elimelech got up and approached the man, who had just finished the last scraps of his meal. Elimelech sat down opposite him and began to talk to him. Aharon and Bentzion gazed at them, entranced. The warm, heartfelt way Elimelech treated the poor Jew left the two students completely absorbed in the scene that was at once fascinating yet strange.

"We need to catch Elimelech some time for a conversation," Aharon whispered to Bentzion, as they got up from the table. "He must be very interesting, really hiding his true nature."

Bentzion nodded in agreement, and added, "I'm sure that that Jew, too, has an interesting tale behind him. We should ask Elimelech about that later."

"I'm not sure he'll agree to tell us about him," Aharon responded. "Elimelech is not an ordinary boy."

This conversation bonded Aharon and Bentzion in a secret way, as if an alliance had been formed between them. Aharon started to feel that Bentzion was someone after his own heart.

Bentzion's usual bubbly cheer and enthusiasm did not frighten Aharon away. On the contrary, he thought to himself, he'll be a perfect balance to my reserve and composure. When he offered Bentzion to become his study partner, the arrangement seemed obvious to both of them, as if it was something perfectly natural. The whole class was amazed, but Aharon and Bentzion knew that, beyond all their differences, they shared something in common that was deep and intrinsic.

They became fast friends in heart and soul, hiding nothing from each other. They encouraged each other, spurred each other on, and even scolded each other. Together they debated all kinds of issues. Together they sought to find their path to serving *Hashem*.

"Dovid and Yehonasan" was how their classmates referred to the pair!

One day Aharon reminded Bentzion about their decision to find out more about Elimelech. "Look how Elimelech conceals himself," Aharon pointed out. "We spoke about trying to find out what he's hiding, but his conduct makes everyone forget about him. Tonight I'm going to try to get into conversation with him in the library. He'll be there for sure."

"Good luck," Bentzion wished him.

CHAPTER THREE
A SEARCHING SOUL

It was 1:00 a.m. Most lights in the *beis hamedrash* were already closed. Only a few students still sat there but they seemed about to leave. This was the hour Aharon had awaited. Although his *Gemara* was still open, his thoughts were on the nearby library room where Elimelech sat, as always, perusing its treasures.

A thin shaft of light shone from the library into the darkening *beis hamedrash*. Impatiently, Aharon waited for the other students to leave until he and Elimelech would be the only ones remaining, reasoning it would be easier to start a conversation with him with no one else around.

But he was starting to feel nervous. Previously he had imagined it would be straightforward to talk to Elimelech; he would simply approach him and start talking to him. Now, however, as the moment was coming closer, he began to wonder how to start a conversation with him. Trying to dismiss his growing anxiety, he asked himself why he was so nervous. Why make such a big deal about starting a conversation with a boy his own age?

Thinking about it, he had to ask himself what he had in common with Elimelech. Rarely had he had any reason or opportunity to speak to him. Their few exchanges had been limited to practical questions and answers or conversations related to their study subjects. A certain distance had always remained between them. Never had they talked freely like friends, so how could he just approach him now?

After a while, Aharon guessed that no one was still left in the library beside Elimelech. He still had no idea what to say, but decided to take the plunge. It would be easier to start talking, he reckoned, as soon as he made eye contact with Elimelech.

Almost on tiptoe, he entered the library. As usual, Elimelech sat near the bookshelves of *mussar* (traditional works of ethics), *Chassidus*, and *Kabbala*, his head resting on one hand and his eyes immersed in the book in front of him. Aharon randomly chose a book from the shelves and sat in a good spot near Elimelech's table, watching him discreetly. Although he pretended to read the book he had taken, his eyes looked up every few moments to glance at Elimelech. Desperately he tried to think of how to approach him.

***

Suddenly, Aharon noticed a pleased, uplifted look appearing on Elimelech's face. He would give anything to discover what was happening in Elimelech's mind to give him such inner happiness.

In fact, Elimelech had just discovered, in the introduction of a book he had opened, the answer to a question long bothering him. Amazing, he thought to himself, how a person can search for something everywhere, without success. And then, without even realizing how it happens, what he has sought for so long falls into his hands, straight from Heaven, when he least expects it!

Ever since Elimelech had decided to seek his personal path for serving *Hashem* and had started to work on refining himself, a major question had bothered him. Why does one need to spend so much time and effort on rectifying character traits and refining one's body? Why spend time learning about the soul's inner workings, about the evil inclination's machinations and one's underlying desires? Surely, as our Sages say, *Hashem* promises, "I have created the *yetzer hara* (evil inclination), and I have created Torah as its antidote"? Accordingly, just dedication to Torah study should be enough to refine one's character traits, to overcome one's baser tendencies, and to lead one onto the true path!

The question bothered him not just because of his curious nature. It resulted from a deep inner struggle that would not leave him. Often, it disturbed his peace of mind, giving him the sense that all his efforts and late-night hours spent studying works of *mussar* and *Chassidus* were just an attempt to cover his insufficient diligence in Torah study. If only he would devote himself entirely to Torah study, he berated himself, he would not need all these works of *mussar* and *Chassidus*, and all this effort he invested in them would be unnecessary. Perhaps these subjects were intended only for those not completely devoted to Torah study. Only someone whose mind is distracted by matters other than Torah would need to toil at the inner spiritual labor taught in works of *mussar* and *Chassidus*. But surely someone whose entire world is Torah study should lack nothing else, for the Torah itself will set him on the right path.

Intuitively, he realized that this is not correct, that it's insufficient to study Talmud and *Halacha* alone. Something else is surely necessary. Everyone needs to find some path in serving *Hashem*. But his mind sought a clear, logical explanation that would provide an irrefutable answer.

Now, right here in the small book he had opened, it was as if *Hashem* had handed him directly the explanation he sought. Its introduction stated that indeed, in earlier generations, such books of introspection and service of G-d were unnecessary, because those generations' souls were holy and lofty, enabling them to find, in the *Gemara* and the works of the *Rishonim* (medieval Torah authorities), everything needed to serve *Hashem* perfectly. Those generations also felt the G-dly light in *Nigleh* – the revealed Torah, Talmud and *Halacha* – and when they studied it, that light illuminated their soul and refined their body and baser inclinations.

In later generations, however, our minds and hearts have become diminished, and the material world has become much coarser, to the point that it has become far more difficult, even impossible, to feel the G-dly light though study of *Nigleh* alone. Ordinary people, the introduction emphasized, have difficulty finding just in normal Torah study the right path for serving *Hashem*.

Therefore it is now necessary to study works of *mussar* that inspire awe of *Hashem*, so that one can find peace for his soul that thirsts to serve *Hashem* properly. Only through such works can these later generations come to feel, while studying *Gemara* too, the G-dly light and to sense that it is *Hashem*'s Torah.

The introduction brought an analogy to clarify this: the difference between one who is healthy and one who is sick. A healthy person needs no food other than bread, meat, and water, for ordinary food is sufficient for his body to get whatever it needs to be perfectly healthy. For somone sick, on the other hand, ordinary food is insufficient. He needs special medications to heal his sickness. If he doesn't receive the required medications and eats only what a healthy person eats, his sickness will get worse until he is unable to eat even bread and meat.

So it is regarding successive generations. The earlier ones were like healthy people; it was enough for them to study *Nigleh*. But the later generations are like sick people, who need medications – spiritual therapies in the form of *mussar* works that inspire awe of *Hashem*. If someone in our time claims to be like earlier generations, saying that study of Talmud and *Halacha* is sufficient for him, it can easily happen, as our Sages have said, that studying Torah in a manner that "he has no merit, it becomes for him a deadly poison," G-d forbid.

Elimelech was elated. He had not expected such a simple, clear explanation. Glancing at the title page, he noticed its year of publication: 5546 (1786). Amazingly, two and a half centuries ago, in the generation of the Vilna Gaon and other Torah giants, they had warned not to study Torah alone without refining one's character and materiality by studying *mussar* works that inspire us with awe of *Hashem*, even writing that such study on its own could become a deadly poison. What then should we say today? Can we imagine in our times that it is possible to be a perfect Jew, serving G-d with perfection, without studying those works and toiling to fulfill their prescriptions?

✳✳✳

All this time, Aharon had been observing Elimelech. He had immediately noticed the elation that lit up his face as soon as he read through that passage. Elimelech's face shone with an inner light, and Aharon realized that something spiritual had happened.

Aharon felt a sudden fondness for Elimelech and his secretiveness. Elimelech's gentle face clearly reflected his inner world. Feeling now closer to him, Aharon felt his previous fear of talking to him melting away, for he sensed that Elimelech would accept him happily.

Without further thought, Aharon got up and slowly approached Elimelech. "I would like to talk to you a little," he said.

Aharon's approach interrupted Elimelech's thoughts. But he replied with an inviting smile, "Please, come sit down."

As Aharon took a seat opposite Elimelech, he realized this was the first time he was looking at him from so close. Until now, he had recognized Elimelech in a vague, distant sort of way. Now that he was sitting just a few inches away, he observed him intently, noticing Elimelech's shining eyes, full of sensitivity, that seemed to express both joy and sadness. At one moment they seemed to show pain, turmoil and hesitation, and a moment later, joy, wholesomeness and happiness. His smile was natural, warm, and sincere, to the extent that the warmth filled Aharon's heart, too.

For a few moments, he just sat there gazing at Elimelech. Suddenly he realized he had to say something. He decided to tell him the truth, sharing what he had come to discuss with full honesty.

"As I understand," Aharon said, "you've found a unique way of serving *Hashem*. You're different from the rest of us. You behave differently, you organize your day differently, you're involved in other things." Aharon searched for the right words. "I'm just very interested in finding out what's at the root of it..."

"Wow, those are big words you're saying!" Elimelech laughed. "A unique way of serving G-d! I haven't found any way. Actually, I'm still searching. I feel I'm missing something, and I'm searching for it."

"What do you mean you're missing?" Aharon probed. "What are you referring to?"

"The problem is that I myself don't know what it is I'm missing," Elimelech replied. "It's hard to define. I'm missing some sort of clarity, a sense of satisfaction and perfection."

"Isn't that why we study Torah," asked Aharon. "The more we study, the more we understand. The more we devote ourselves to Torah study, the more we're inspired and uplifted."

"Yes, that's the question," Elimelech told him, deep in thought. "Is it possible to suffice with what we're studying here in yeshiva? Is it really enough? It seems to me that something else is also necessary."

"To tell you the truth," Aharon said, "such thoughts put me off. Of course, we all want to advance to higher levels of spirituality. But I suspect that the tendency to seek various mysterious paths is just a way to escape from the true challenge, the hard work of studying Torah. I think that when we learn properly, we don't need anything else."

Elimelech did not respond right away. Aharon's words reminded him of himself. In the past he too had deliberated on exactly these thoughts. He recalled the long nights he had sat alone in the library, torn apart by the inner battle raging in his mind.

He was not offended by Aharon's words. On the contrary, he

understood him well. He was even happy to be given a chance to talk about it. He was even happier that this conversation was occurring exactly at that moment, right after he had found the clear answer that had so eased his troubled thoughts.

Meanwhile, however, Aharon was dismayed by Elimelech's silence. He was afraid his words had been out of place and had hurt him. Perhaps what he had said would cut short their conversation with hard feelings, forestalling forever the chance to continue it.

"I'm sorry if I've insulted you," he pleaded, trying to restore the pleasant spirit of moments ago. "I didn't mean to attack you. I really do want to understand."

"No, don't be silly," Elimelech replied, "it's just that you reminded me of something. Actually, I understand you very well. I, too, have felt a lot of confusion on this issue."

"So what is your perspective on the topic?" Aharon asked.

"If you want," Elimelech said, "I can tell you about one of the thoughts that bothered me, which convinced me that something else must be necessary besides studying *Gemara* and its commentaries. Look, there are subjects to which we never give a moment's thought until the bitter truth suddenly flashes through our mind that we've never approached certain fundamental subjects with due seriousness.

"Take something simple," Elimelech continued. "The words we say several times a day in *Sh'ma*, 'You shall love *Hashem*, your G-d, with all your heart and all your soul and all your might.' When we say this verse while reading the *Sh'ma*, we force ourselves, in an artificial way, to feel some sort of vague feeling, and we call that 'love of *Hashem*'...

"But if we're honest with ourselves, is that 'love'? Does this vague feeling have the least similarity to the real love that fills our hearts towards our parents, siblings, and friends? When we're in yeshiva, away from home for a few weeks, we feel homesick, we miss our parents terribly. Why? Because we love them. Do we also long for *Hashem* like that?"

"Fine," Aharon answered. "You can't compare the two. *Hashem* is an abstract existence. We have no way of understanding or grasping Him with our senses. What do you want, that we should love *Hashem*, who is transcendent and higher than our understanding, in the same way we love our parents who gave birth to us? Love of *Hashem* is a different kind of love."

"For sure, it is a different kind of love," Elimelech responded. "But if we would stop deceiving ourselves and just reflect on the matter for even a moment, we would conclude that what we call 'love of *Hashem*' is basically a joke. When you love someone, you are drawn to him, you think about him, you want to be near him. That's the common denominator of all kinds of love. But when we talk about 'love of *Hashem*,' I think if we lose some object it bothers us more than our relationship with *Hashem*!"

"I'm not sure that you're correct," Aharon said. "I need to think about it more. But assuming you're right, what's the point you're trying to make?"

"Think about it," said Elimelech. "The problem is that people don't think about it altogether. I'll explain the point I'm trying to make. Loving *Hashem* is a *mitzva* of the Torah. So it must apply to all of us. If so, how is it possible to come to true love of *Hashem*?"

"I don't know what to tell you," Aharon answered, hesitating. "One would think that when we study the Torah and see *Hashem*'s great wisdom revealed in it, we begin to feel true love for Him."

"That's true," Elimelech agreed. "But to feel love for *Hashem* through Torah study, we need, while we're actually studying it, to feel that it's *Hashem*'s Torah. The problem is that while we're studying Torah, we're more focused on the wisdom within it, on explanations of its details, so that we're too busy to feel it's *Hashem*'s Torah."

"And so?" Aharon questioned.

"So that proves that something else is necessary," Elimelech said. "That's what I meant when I said it's not enough to study *Gemara*, and that something else is necessary, too."

"And what's that something else?" Aharon asked.

"Well, now we're going back to where we started," Elimelech smiled. "Actually, I don't yet know exactly what that something is. In all my searching until now, I've discovered that it has to include two aspects. First, there has to be some way to purify and refine the body and the natural tendencies. That's because, when the body and character traits are coarse, it's impossible to sense feelings of holiness. So that comes first. But besides that, it's also necessary to learn about the greatness of the Creator. Without learning about *Hashem*, He'll remain an abstract figure in our imagination, to Whom we have no connection. Studying about *Hashem*'s greatness brings us closer to Him."

"Where did you find all these ideas?" Aharon wanted to know.

"Since this subject started bothering me," Elimelech explained, "I began reading various Torah works. I've read lots of works of *mussar* and *Chassidus*. I've taken a point from here and another from there, gradually clarifying many concepts for myself. But I haven't yet achieved complete clarity."

"You mentioned books of *Chassidus*," Aharon said. "In fact, I've never tried looking into them. I'm familiar with some *mussar* works, but not with *Chassidus*. What's special about it?"

"I can't yet give you a proper answer," Elimelech sighed. "But it seems to me that the difference between the path of *mussar* and the path of *Chassidus* is that *mussar* emphasizes breaking the body and the *yetzer hara*, while *Chassidus* emphasizes the greatness of *Hashem*. That's why *mussar* tends to make one feel downhearted, while *Chassidus* has a spirit of joy and exhilaration. I don't know which path is preferable. I have a feeling that both are needed."

The first light of dawn was coming through the windows, and Aharon glanced at his watch. He realized the night was almost over.

"It's so late," Aharon said. "We really should try to catch some sleep."

They both got up. Elimelech returned his books to their shelves and closed the lights as daylight started to fill the room.

Silently, the two walked to the dorm, each lost in his thoughts.

The conversation had given both much to think about. Aharon wanted to digest it, planning to discuss it with Bentzion.

"Good night, or rather, good morning," he said to Elimelech, as they reached their bedrooms. "I'd like to continue this conversation at some time."

"Whenever you like," Elimelech responded, with a warm, friendly smile. "I think this conversation has helped me a lot, too, to clarify these ideas for myself."

CHAPTER FOUR
A CHASSIDISHE *FARBRENGEN*

During their lunch break later that day, Aharon told Bentzion about his conversation with Elimelech.

"What impressed me most of all was his sincere, straightforward approach to the topic," he reflected. "He didn't play with words. In his mind, whatever is true in theory has to translate into practice. We're commanded to love *Hashem,* so he's concerned how to achieve it."

"That's an interesting point," said Bentzion. "We're all aware of these issues and agree that that's how it should be, but there's this feeling that somehow they don't apply to us but only to high-level *tzaddikim.* Very few people actually take all this seriously."

"And we're not yet even counted among those few!" Aharon pointed out.

"You know, something must have occurred in Elimelech's life that has never happened to us," Bentzion rationalized. "I've no doubt that Elimelech's attitude must have come as a result of some event that shook him up. Without such an .experience, people don't usually change."

"Why waste time guessing? When I get a chance, I'll try and ask him whether he ever had such an experience," Aharon decided. "In any case, we needn't wait for some such experience to shock us into changing ourselves. We're not animals who understand

37

only the language of compulsion. We have a mind and free choice to follow whatever our mind feels it has to do."

"I hope you're right," Bentzion murmured.

***

A whole week passed after Aharon's late-night conversation with Elimelech. Outwardly, nothing changed. Elimelech continued keeping to himself, staying far from his classmates' social life. Aharon, too, continued his routine. Someone who paid extra attention might have noticed a certain degree of warmth between the two as they nodded at each other on passing through the hallway. Beyond that, however, no special connection was apparent between them.

Their next conversation started as if by accident. A well-known Torah fund in Yerushalayim decided to award scholarships to many yeshivos, and asked each to send representatives to be tested in order to determine how to distribute the scholarships. The *Rosh Yeshiva* didn't need much deliberation to decide whom to select as his yeshiva's representatives. The natural choices were Aharon and Elimelech. Within days the two were sitting together on a bus to Yerushalayim.

At first they discussed the test they would be taking. Then Aharon found an opportunity to continue their previous conversation.

"Our discussion last time gave me much to think about," he told Elimelech. "I must say that now I agree with everything you said. But I'd like to know what made you start thinking about all this? Did you come to it as a result of some passing thought, or perhaps something happened that made you change?"

"You're right," Elimelech smiled. "Very few people escape the rhythm of their life to realize how they haven't been giving serious thought to such basic ideas. We usually need some outside stimulus to shake us up in order to open our eyes."

"So what happened in your case?" Aharon asked.

"I'll tell you," Elimelech answered. "Last winter I was home in Haifa for a few days for some medical tests I needed. One evening, as I walked home from *Maariv*, I saw a car stop near a nearby *shul*, and an older man got out, accompanied by a few younger men.

"The older man looked really impressive, with striking features. With one of those typical Russian caps on his head, he had a long, broad white beard. His face shone with intelligence, and his eyes were pure but penetrating, reflecting great power and determination, but also gentle warmth. I gathered that he must be some sort of Rebbe.

"They went into the *shul*, and out of curiosity I followed. Inside, a few dozen men sat around a table awaiting him. Some were Chassidim of various groups, as one could see from their typical clothing. Others were Litvaks – non-Chassidic Orthodox Jews. Others seemed more modern, wearing knitted *kipot* on their heads, while others seemed to have no particular affiliation. That surprised me, because Chassidim who follow a Rebbe are usually similar to each other in dress and manner, whereas here were all kinds of Jews.

"When this Jew entered the *shul*, everyone stood up respectfully, walking over to greet him with a warm '*sholom aleichem.*' He and those accompanying him washed their hands for eating bread and joined everyone else at the table.

"It must be some sort of *seudas mitzva*, I thought. But soon I realized it couldn't be. The refreshments on the table were not what would be served at a *seudas mitzva*. Any self-respecting person would be embarrassed to serve such a simple meal. The actual plates were simple. On them was sliced black bread, herring, and pickles, plus a few bowls of vegetable salad, a bottle of vodka – really a poor man's meal.

"It all piqued my interest. I sat at the end of the table to watch. The impressive Jew, whom everyone called Reb Dovid Leib, poured a shot-glass of vodka for himself, and wished everyone *'l'chayim!'* Everyone responded, *'l'chayim v'liv'rocha!'* Reb Dovid Leib drank half the glass and called on them, 'What are you waiting for? Say *l'chayim!*' One of them poured vodka into many shot-glasses and passed them around, and meanwhile everyone started to sing.

"Their songs were mostly unfamiliar to me. Some were upbeat and happy, while others were slow, calming, and thought-provoking. Reb Dovid Leib's enthusiasm gradually grew, as he occasionally struck the table to the beat of the tune and sang with all his soul, his eyes closed, his deeply creased face expressing intense concentration.

"The songs created a certain mood of seriousness and depth, even holiness. You felt yourself rising above the pettiness of everyday life and reaching an exalted spiritual world. Despite being an outsider, I didn't felt at all uncomfortable or out of place. The spirit felt warm and inclusive.

"I asked the man next to me who Reb Dovid Leib was. He answered simply, 'He's the *Mashpia*.' I was going to ask what that means but just then Reb Dovid Leib began speaking.

"The whole scene was unique, a type of gathering totally unfamiliar to most of us. Some things seemed strange and different, such as drinking vodka, the simple food, the unusual type of meal. But the heart-rousing songs, Reb Dovid's impressive features and his quiet words all turned that meal, at least for me, into something truly special."

"It sounds like stories of old-time Europe," Aharon observed.

"I thought of that," Elimelech agreed. "But you'll be surprised to hear it still exists, and for those sitting there it seemed nothing unusual. The man next to me told me they often hold such gatherings, which they call *farbrengens*."

"But I still don't understand what changed you," Aharon probed.

"I'm getting to that," Elimelech answered. "Until now, I've described only the general atmosphere. What really struck me was what Reb Dovid Leib said.

"He based his words on what our Sages say at the end of *Gemara Kiddushin*, 'I was created to serve my Creator.' Another version of this saying is, 'I was created **only** to serve my Creator.' And he explained at length the difference between the two versions.

"The first version, 'I was created to serve my Creator,' leaves room to say that while our main purpose in the world is to serve *Hashem*, along with that we have the option of enjoying this world – within Torah guidelines, of course – and to seek various material goals for our own benefit. The second version, however, leaves nothing in this world besides serving our Creator, as it says, 'I was created **only** to serve my Creator,' meaning that if not for serving *Hashem*, there's no reason for our creation. The sole reason we were created is to serve our Creator.

"That was Reb Dovid's Leib's starting point. He explained that obviously there's no disagreement between the two versions. The second version only clarifies and explains the first version. So man's sole purpose on this earth is to serve our Creator.

"Reb Dovid Leib showed great talent for explaining everything in an ironic and witty way. He described a certain 'fictional' personality, at whose expense we all smiled while he spoke. Only afterwards did we grasp that we were really laughing at ourselves.

"He described a G-d-fearing Jew who is careful in every detail of *Halacha*, a learned scholar who spends all day studying Torah. Such a Jew clearly earns his reward in both this world and the next. He rises very early every morning to study Torah in depth until daybreak. Then he goes to *Shacharis*, praying devotedly and thinking of the words' meaning. After a small breakfast he continues studying Torah until noon, when he eats a satisfying lunch, takes a short nap, and goes back to Torah study until the evening.

"For sure he has a portion in the 'World to Come.' Who can compare to him! *Hashem* praises him before His heavenly court and His heavenly angels. *Moshiach*'s future feast of the *shor habor* and the *livyoson* awaits him on silver platters!

"But he also has this world. He thinks to himself, '*Boruch Hashem*, I've studied and served *Hashem* all day. Now I deserve to enjoy His world!' His wife brings him a generous portion of ice cream, and as he sits on his porch, breathing the evening air and imbibing the cold dessert with pleasure, he thinks, 'How fortunate are we, how good is our portion! Who is like your people Yisroel?'"

Listening to this last part, Aharon felt annoyed. The apparent mockery at the expense of a Torah scholar really bothered him. "You say you were laughing. I'm sure I wouldn't have laughed. It's worse than just making fun of Torah scholars!"

"Believe me, I've spent much time thinking about it since then," Elimelech said. "Look, when Reb Dovid spoke, you could see the truth radiating from him and the holiness enveloping him. You couldn't have attributed to him any mockery of Torah scholars. When I retell it, my voice may sound a little scornful, but when he spoke, it sounded entirely different."

"To me it sounds disturbing," Aharon said, "and I wouldn't have wanted to hear such words."

"You know, it's possible that the exaggerated depiction seems a little insulting," Elimelech conceded. "But let's try to ignore the depiction and just focus on his intent and content. It's possible that if Reb Dovid Leib had not provided an exaggerated, humorous illustration, his words would not have been grasped clearly enough."

"Okay, continue," Aharon said.

"And so," Elimelech continued, "Reb Dovid Leib described the personality of a Jew who studies Torah, prays devotedly, observes *mitzvos* perfectly, but despite this maintains two separate areas in his life, at least in a subtle manner. He dedicates so much time to *Hashem*, but also feels he deserves something for it. He too exists as an entity and feels entitled to some benefit.

"That was Reb Dovid Leib's first talk. He said '*l'chayim*' again, and the others responded with their own '*l'chayim*.'" They started singing a profound melody which they called 'The *Beinoni*.' The man next to me explained that this melody reflects the inner personality of someone who's at the high level called a '*beinoni*,' but he didn't explain what exactly a '*beinoni*' is.

"They must have sung that melody about ten times, with deeper and deeper feeling, without anyone feeling bored or any sense of repetition. Their melodies in general, I must say, are deeply inspiring, and I began to understand why song has such an important place in the world of *Chassidus*. Songs, apparently, can express and communicate no less than words.

"When they finished singing, Reb Dovid Leib continued the same topic, but this time shifting perspective. He described a Jewish businessman, busy all day at work, who nevertheless sets time for Torah study and even prays with concentration, as much as time allows.

"Here again, Reb Dovid Leib showed how the two areas of his life remain distinct. When he studies and prays, his mind and heart are full of holy thoughts and he feels he's serving *Hashem*. But when he goes to work, he feels disconnected from his service of *Hashem* and the holiness he felt while praying and studying – as happens to most people.

"Of course, while involved in business, he's careful to avoid forbidden talk such as gossip, and he avoids any dishonesty. But he views his business as an area of life essentially separate from *Hashem*. He feels, however, that he has no choice but to work, because he has to make a living. He doesn't see his job as part of serving *Hashem*..."

"Well, of course," Aharon interjected. "Is doing business or bargaining with a customer over the price of merchandise a holy service of *Hashem*? How could you think differently?"

"That exact thought passed through my mind when Reb Dovid Leib finished that part of his talk and they started singing again," Elimelech told Aharon. "But as soon as he started speaking again, I realized what he meant. And it was his final words that totally changed my world.

"He told about a certain *Chassid* in Europe several generations ago who was a successful lumber merchant, doing business in many cities and dealing with enormous sums. Once, after hours of balancing his accounts, calculating and writing down all the numbers, as he finally arrived at the total, he drew a line under everything and wrote, '*ein od milvado* – there's nothing else beside Him!'

"The story seems amusing. But Reb Dovid Leib explained it. That *Chassid* was a true servant of *Hashem* in all areas of his life. For him, even his business dealings were part of his service of *Hashem*. He fulfilled the directive of the verse, '*bechol derochecha do'eihu* – know Him in all your ways' – that in every deed and area of life, we should serve *Hashem*. When we go to work, we shouldn't feel it's separate from holiness. Even there we should continue to serve *Hashem*. It's just that our service of *Hashem* then takes a different form; previously we served *Hashem* through Torah study and in prayer, and now we serve Him by doing business.

"To summarize," Elimelech concluded, "those words suddenly opened a whole new world for me. I realized that the concept of 'I was created only to serve my Creator' is not so simple. We study, we pray, we fulfill the *mitzvos*, but we don't feel that our whole existence and purpose in this world is to serve *Hashem* because there's nothing else besides Him.

"The *farbrengen* ended at about 1:00 a.m. As I walked out of the *shul*, I felt I'd been exposed to a whole new approach to the Torah and its *mitzvos*, an approach utterly unfamiliar to me before. I realized how little I knew about true, authentic service of *Hashem*. It brought me to the conclusion that I need to take it into my own hands and start to search."

"So, have you found what you were looking for?" Aharon smiled.

"I've found out a lot more than I knew before," Elimelech declared with a serious expression. "Since then I've opened a window to worlds I never dreamed existed. But, as I told you, I still haven't discovered the clarity I felt so keenly that night in Haifa. And I get the feeling that the journey to get there is still a long one."

CHAPTER FIVE
A WORLD WITHIN A WORLD

The Three Weeks of mourning for the *Beis Hamikdash*, concluding with the fast of *Tisha B'av*, come at the end of the yeshivos' school year, when the students leave to spend their short summer break at home. Elimelech went back to Haifa, planning to take full advantage of his vacation. As a result of his long conversations with Aharon, he had lately been lagging in his schedule of private study on the spiritual subjects so dear to him. Now he intended to utilize the time to make up what he had missed.

Lately, however, their conversations had started to trouble him. On the one hand, he appreciated Aharon's straightforward manner, and his desire to get to the heart of every concept. He was impressed to see how seriously his friend took his words, and how the subjects they discussed were starting to animate him more and more. On the other hand, the more their conversations developed, the more problems seemed to appear. Every conversation forced Elimelech to expose his inner world to an extent he was not too eager to do. Bringing someone else into his mental space and sharing his thoughts and hesitations were giving him a growing feeling of discomfort.

On its own, though, that was tolerable. Seeing how his words made such an impression on Aharon, helping him to grow in Torah study and service of *Hashem*, allowed Elimelech to put up with the difficulty of sacrificing his personal privacy to benefit his friend.

What bothered him much more was a growing distance between their points of view. It was becoming more and more obvious to Elimelech that his way of thinking differed greatly from his friend's. During the months that Elimelech had absorbed so many ideas from the works of *Chassidus* he had studied, they had become part of his being. Now he started to realize just how different his approach was from Aharon's.

For example, Elimelech related to prayer as a way to connect with and become united with *Hashem*. For him, prayer was the time when one can leave the confines of ordinary existence and interests to try to become uplifted and united with *Hashem*. The very word *tefila* (prayer), he had learned from Chassidic works, derives from the word in the Halachic phrase, *hatofeil klei cheres* ("one who joins earthenware vessels"), implying that prayer means "joining and uniting."

For Aharon, however, prayer is mainly for the purpose of asking for one's needs, a time when one is received by the Divine King and can request what he desires. Of course, a yeshiva student does not ask for his cow to give milk but for success in Torah study, for inspiration to repent properly, and for the welfare of the Jewish people in general. But the main point of prayer for him was to ask for fulfillment of personal desires. Often Elimelech felt as if they were talking to each other in two different languages.

He couldn't look down on Aharon for this attitude, for he remembered how, not long ago, he too had thought that way. It was only because, to his good fortune, Elimelech had been privileged to chance upon that *farbrengen* in Haifa when he had heard Reb Dovid Leib tell two stories that inspired him to see the concept of prayer in an entirely different, loftier light.

The first story was about an outstanding follower of the *Baal HaTanya*. The *Chassid* was a great Torah scholar who prayed with great fervor. On the other hand, he was also witty and clever, with a rare talent for performing "pranks" and saying incisive witticisms to inspire those around him to serve *Hashem* with greater devotion.

Once, during the days of *Selichos* – the prayers said before *Rosh Hashana* to plead with *Hashem* for forgiveness – this *Chassid* was traveling and had stayed over in a small village at an inn owned by an elderly couple. In the middle of the night, the hostess knocked at his door to wake him to accompany them to *shul* for *Selichos*.

"*Selichos*?" he asked. "What's that?"

The hostess was astounded. She whispered to her husband, "It's so strange. An elderly Jew, who looks like a Torah scholar, doesn't even know what *Selichos* are!"

"*Selichos*," she explained to the *Chassid*, "are prayers we say at night in *shul*, to beg *Hashem* that our fields should yield good crops, our cattle should have good grass to graze, our cows and goats should give plenty of milk, and we should have enough food during the coming year."

"That's *Selichos*?" asked the *Chassid*, making a grimace. "Old people wake up in the middle of the night to cry for food? How disgraceful!"

The hostess was embarrassed and at loss for an answer. Seeing how his words had touched her so deeply that she now realized that could not be what *Selichos* are truly about, the *Chassid* explained the inner meaning of *Selichos*, how we are actually weeping over the exile of the *Shechina* (Divine Presence) and over our coarse materiality that prevents us from feeling *Hashem*'s light during our prayers all year long. **That**'s the meaning of *Selichos*!

Following that story, Reb Dovid Leib had told another one, from his personal experience. During the years of the Communist regime in the Soviet Union, the secret police had been in hot pursuit of him simply because he was a Torah-observant Jew. Forced to flee, he wandered across that vast land for several years, hiding in many different communities. Every year he prayed on *Rosh Hashana* and *Yom Kippur* with a different *minyan* of Jews.

"I noticed something very interesting," Reb Dovid Leib related. "In ordinary *shuls*, the congregation's fervor reached its height, their cries from the depths of their hearts rising to the very Heavens, when they said the words, 'Repentance, prayer, and charity remove the evil decree.' In Chassidic *shuls*, on the other hand, the congregation's intensity reached its height and they invested their very life's blood, expressing the innermost desire of their souls, when saying the words, 'You are the living and eternal King'!

"That difference is no coincidence," Reb Dovid Leib explained. "It's a direct result of the special light that the Baal Shem Tov and his disciples revealed, the light that illuminates the concepts of Torah, prayer, *mitzvos* and service of *Hashem*.

"It's true," Reb Dovid Leib continued to clarify, "that the purpose of prayer on *Rosh Hashana* is to request one's personal needs, as Halachic authorities state. It's a time given to us to pour out our hearts before the King of all kings to beg for our needs and desires. Heaven forbid that one should deny this fundamental aspect of prayer.

"At the same time, however, one needs to realize that it is only one aspect, the lowest level, of prayer. The loftier aspect of prayer is to become united with *Hashem*. Prayer is the time when one's soul becomes united with its Divine source, filled with love for *Hashem* and a powerful desire to become one with Him, just as a candle's flame quivers as it yearns to separate from its wick and return to its Heavenly source. This process includes many levels, depending on how well one succeeds in leaving his limitations to become connected with *Hashem*. Generally speaking, though, it's the higher aspect of prayer.

"This point expresses one of the greatest innovations of *Chassidus*," Reb Dovid Leib had emphasized. "Throughout the generations, there have always been great Jews whose prayers have been much more than just requests for their needs. But they were exceptions to the rule, special, exalted individuals, not from the masses. The Baal Shem Tov, on the other hand, through his teachings of *Chassidus*, accomplished that even an ordinary Jew who is not a full-time Torah student, but is busy all day making a living and concerned how to support his family, even he, when he prays, can focus mainly on the higher aspect of prayer, on uniting his soul with *Hashem*, far more than he focuses on asking for his needs.

"A person's focus when he prays is clearly seen when we pay attention to the words he says with the most passion! He may not show so much emotion when he recites the *brocha* of *Refo'einu* (the blessing requesting healing) or *Boreich oleinu* (the blessing asking for livelihood). On the other hand, during *P'sukei d'Zimra* (the earlier part of *Shacharis* praising *Hashem*'s greatness in the world), and particularly during the *brochos* said before and after *Sh'ma*, then you can truly see the yearnings of his soul. When he says the words, 'How great are Your works, *Hashem*! How deep are Your thoughts!' or 'With His goodness He renews every day the work of creation,' he closes his eyes with deep devotion to *Hashem* and completely forgets himself and his problems. His soul melts from the Divine greatness expressed in these verses.

"Again," Reb Dovid Leib repeated, "this does not refer only to special holy people, of whom there may be a handful in a generation. I'm referring to an ordinary person, a *Chassid* who sits and prays, but really **prays**. He forgets all his troubles and life's difficulties and his thoughts are invested in a single concept – *Hashem*'s greatness. That is the great innovation of the Baal Shem Tov and his holy disciples and of the teachings of *Chassidus*!"

Elimelech had decided not to tell Aharon about that part of the *farbrengen*, suspecting he would find it difficult to accept. He still recalled the many thoughts that troubled him for weeks after that *farbrengen*. On the one hand, he felt the exalted nature of the world Reb Dovid Leib had described. His soul sensed it was a lofty world that he could not yet grasp, yet a world he found most appealing and attractive. On the other hand, that world's novelty and unfamiliarity bothered him. If it's all so simple and beautiful, why hadn't he heard about it until then? If it's as Reb

Dovid Leib said, that this beautiful path is available for every individual, why hadn't he been educated in it? And although it did sound so appealing and inspiring, it seemed to uproot the accepted meaning of prayer, replacing it with a whole new meaning.

It took Elimelech a long time to appreciate the concept properly. But he sensed that one who understood it would get to appreciate it, whereas one who did not understand could not easily be convinced of its truth. In any case, he certainly could not be the one to convince anyone as yet, which was why he did not want to discuss it with Aharon.

Bothering him even more was Aharon's cold dismissal of *Chassidus*. Whenever Elimelech mentioned *Chassidus*, he detected the scorn in Aharon's reply. His attitude reminded him of those who claimed that the only advantage of *Chassidus* was to lift the spirits of women and the unlearned. Elimelech was pained at Aharon's blindness to the great light within these teachings.

As soon as Elimelech realized this attitude Aharon had, he started choosing his words more carefully, making sure to mention *Chassidus* as little as possible. Actually, many spiritual ideas he found in works of *Chassidus* reminded him of ideas he had seen in non-Chassidic works, too, so he tried opening Aharon's mind to that spiritual world. He made a point of emphasizing to him how worthwhile it is for every Jew to become acquainted with the wider world of traditional spiritual concepts taught by great Torah leaders of all backgrounds. Seek inspiration, he told him, from all Torah-true sources, because each has its unique quality, and only all of them together can complement each other to create a perfect whole. Despite all his efforts, however, and his many conversations with him, Aharon's view of *Chassidus* barely changed, which pained Elimelech greatly.

Reflecting on it now, he doubted that there was any point in continuing their discussions. Elimelech realized that he himself had not yet formed any clear, permanent viewpoint. At this point, he thought, it would be unwise to get into heated debates with Aharon, especially as Aharon was such a hard nut to crack and would not change his mind easily.

***

A tap on his shoulder woke Elimelech from his reverie. He was surprised to see an old friend, Yonoson, with whom he had studied in *cheder*-school, but who had enrolled at a different *yeshiva ketana* than Elimelech's. Last *Pesach* Yonoson had not been at his home in Haifa, so they had not seen each other for about a year.

Since the last time Elimelech had seen him, Yonoson looked somewhat different. His modern haircut had disappeared, and a sprouting beard now framed his face. Most surprising to Elimelech was a certain refinement apparent on Yonoson's face; he looked transformed, as if the *Shechina*, *Hashem*'s holy presence, rested upon him!

After routine inquiries about each other's welfare, Elimelech became even more surprised. In the past, Yonoson had never seemed to be a profound student with whom one could discuss spiritual subjects such as searching for the truth, or how to serve *Hashem* and come to love Him and feel awe for Him. He had been studious, but sufficed with that, feeling no need for any more.

Elimelech wondered how to explain Yonoson's current interest, and even more, his close familiarity with such spiritual topics. On the one hand, he was delighted to learn how Yonoson had been getting involved in the same issues that had bothered him and was dwelling on similar problems. But what astounded him most was the clarity with which Yonoson was able to analyze and explain the subjects.

Elimelech sensed that during that year when they had not seen each other, Yonoson had achieved what he was still struggling to achieve. Yonoson's clear explanations, his broad and deep understanding, and the simple way he could describe many profound ideas, amazed Elimelech.

He was about to ask Yonoson where this all came from. Meanwhile, though, Yonoson asked him in which *yeshiva gedola* – senior yeshiva – he planned to study in the coming year.

"I'm haven't yet decided," Elimelech said. "What about you?"

"I think I'll be enrolling at *Yeshivas Tom'chei T'mimim* in Kfar Chabad," Yonoson replied.

"Are you serious?" Elimelech was shocked. So that explained why Yonoson seemed so changed. But this begged a larger question. "Why on earth are you going to Chabad?" he asked, utterly overwhelmed. "How did you get there?"

"That's a really long story," Yonoson smiled.

"Does that mean you've become a Chabadnik?" asked Elimelech, by now completely perplexed.

"Not so fast," Yonoson grinned. "One doesn't become a Chabad *Chassid* overnight. It's just that I've found it to be a path that's impossible to ignore, and I'm trying to follow it."

"But how did that happen?" Elimelech struggled to comprehend. "Did you suddenly decide one day, just like that?"

"If you really want to know," Yonoson said, "I'll tell you."

Rumors had reached him about a *Tanya* class, specifically for yeshiva students, which some of his classmates secretly attended. The allure of secrecy, coupled with his natural curiosity, prompted Yonoson to try it out. Soon his curiosity turned into a deep yearning to learn and become familiar with the impressive world of *Chassidus* revealed before him.

"What particularly attracted you?" Elimelech asked.

"For me personally it was the exalted concepts," Yonoson explained. "The whole approach of *Chassidus* provides an utterly different perspective on subjects most of us take for granted. Suddenly you see a whole new world within the world you already know. Things you thought you understood, seemingly so clear and straightforward, now appear in a different light, much more exalted. For the first time, I began to feel how small I am and how naive had been my understanding of everything until now."

"For example," Elimelech urged.

"I can give you countless examples," Yonosan replied. "Let's take the essential nature of the Torah. What is the Torah? For the first time in my life I heard a broad explanation, based on the *Midrash* stating that the Torah is 'an analogy for the Original

Being.' What does that mean? It's an analogy for exalted spiritual levels, which are themselves an analogy for even higher levels, ad infinitum. The RaMBaN, Rabbi Moshe ben Nachman, expressed it as follows, 'Scripture tells us about lower beings, while hinting at higher levels.'

"Another example: *Tanya*'s explanation, derived from the *Kabbala*, of how every Jew has two separate souls – not just two tendencies, the *yetzer tov* and the *yetzer hara*, as we might understand from our Sages, but two actual souls, the *nefesh Elokis* (Divine soul) and the *nefesh habehamis* (animal soul). Based on this revolutionary concept and various sources in the *Gemara*, he explains the meaning of the different levels among Jews of *tzaddik*, *rasha*, and *beinoni*. He explains what 'love of *Hashem*' truly means, and how, if one still has the slightest love for worldly desires, one cannot have true love of *Hashem*, for two loves cannot coexist in one's heart. It was when I learned this that I first grasped the meaning of 'love of *Hashem*'!

"Or, for instance, the seemingly simple words we say every day in our prayers, 'In His goodness he renews, every day constantly, the work of creation.' The second part of *Tanya*, called *Shaar Hayichud V'ha'emuna*, explains in depth the meaning of these words in an amazing way. I was overwhelmed when I understood that it's the G-dly energy that constantly gives existence to every detail and particle in the universe, and that if that energy were removed, G-d forbid, for an instant, everything would immediately cease to exist as if it had never existed. It's astounding! Just think about the implications of this idea. From that single concept emerges a whole new outlook on Divine Providence, and much, much more.

"You just can't remain indifferent in the face of all this," Yonoson concluded, falling silent.

Elimelech stared at him, and a strange feeling filled him. I've been searching for so long for exactly this clarity, he thought, and now the place where I can attain it is presented to me for the taking! What do I have to lose? Go once to attend such a class. If it has changed Yonosan so positively, there must be something to it.

"Where can I find a class like that?" he asked. Yonoson promised to find out, and a few days later came back with a list of classes. Now Elimelech waited impatiently for the end of summer vacation. He had decided he just had to attend a *Tanya* class.

CHAPTER SIX
THE SPECIAL MONTH OF ELUL

The new yeshiva year starts on *Rosh Chodesh* Elul. Aharon and Bentzion had both decided to enroll at the same senior yeshiva, a well-known *yeshiva gedola*. Both realized that their previous three years in *yeshiva ketana* had been, relatively speaking, like child's play compared to the challenge of advanced Torah study they were starting now, which would ultimately define their personal missions in the world. Everything they had accomplished until now had been preparing them for the higher level of Torah study they were entering, when they would get the opportunity to become real Torah scholars.

Together they watched the hundreds of students entering the study hall, hoping to see a familiar face. At the end of the previous school year, many students had not yet decided which *yeshiva gedola* to select for the coming year. With great interest the two companions now waited to see which of last year's fellow students had made the same choice to join this outstanding yeshiva.

The yeshiva *seder* – the official study session – had not yet begun that morning, so the two felt free to immerse themselves in this new experience of becoming students at the *yeshiva gedola*. There was a heightened feeling of awe in this unfamiliar place, observing the new Talmud lecturers and fellow students. There was a sense of novelty in the great hall, of progressing not only to a new place, but also in their personal status. Feeling a new chapter was opening in their lives, the new students were full of good resolutions, for starting one's first year in *yeshiva gedola* was of such great significance.

Aharon shook himself from these pleasant thoughts, as he observed to Bentzion, "Everything goes according to the beginning. The first moment is decisive. I heard from our *Mashgiach* that a whole year can sometimes go to waste for a student just because he lets its first moment pass without utilizing it, by saying to himself, 'I'll start studying in one more minute.' He wants to enjoy the novelty of the new place and get used to it a little. But in that minute, he lets the year get off to a wrong start. So come on, let's start studying!"

This study during those first days had a special charm. Even the weaker students applied themselves to Torah study with immense diligence. The sense of novelty aroused everyone with great enthusiasm to study without any limit, as if nothing was more natural than to study all day long, with total dedication.

"If only we could feel this way all year," Bentzion said to Aharon one evening.

"Don't fall for illusions," Aharon told him with an air of authority. "It's just the feeling of novelty, of breaking out of routine. Woe to anyone who relies on this and forgets about fighting his *yetzer hara*. Before long the thrill will wear off and he'll be in for a rude awakening. One always needs to struggle with his own effort for the inspiration to last. But when someone relies on external incentives, when they eventually disappear he'll experience a fall."

"Not necessarily," Bentzion tried to argue. "Sometimes such a situation can become a turning point in a student's life. He may begin to study enthusiastically because of the novelty, and once he realizes how good it is, he'll continue to study well even after the sense of novelty wears off."

"That's true," Aharon agreed. "But only if he studies not only because of the sense of novelty but also by increasing his diligence on his own steam, by his own decisions. In that case you'd be right, because then the sense of novelty becomes an impetus to advance further, inspiring him to grow stronger and giving him energy to work. But if he relies only on his initial elation, he remains with nothing when this feeling passes."

"That does make some sense," Bentzion conceded. "But is that how it plays out in practice?"

"Of course it is!" Aharon insisted. "I'll give you another example. Sometimes one can suddenly feel inspired with an elated inspiration to serve *Hashem*. He yearns to pray with all his heart, to study Torah diligently, and to work on improving himself. That's called, in many Torah works, *isarusa dil'eila*, 'an awakening from Above,' an inspiration from Heaven. Those sources explain that if you want to hold onto this feeling of inspiration and make it permanent, you need to add to it an *isarusa dil'sata*, 'an awakening from below,' arousing inspiration from within yourself that you develop with your own abilities. That ensures that the inspiration becomes permanent and doesn't evaporate. But if you rely only on the 'awakening from Above,' without investing your own effort into your spiritual growth, then when the inspiration eventually passes, you end up just as you were before."

"You must have heard all that from Elimelech," Bentzion guessed, with a smile.

"You're right," agreed Aharon, smiling back.

Bentzion's mention of Elimelech sent a shiver of emotion through Aharon. Now he understood his recent feeling that he was missing something. He had wondered about this strange feeling. There seemed to be no reason not to be happy. The classes were excellent, his new classmates made a good, positive impression. He certainly had no complaints about his room and board at the new yeshiva. So why did he sometimes feel a sense of loneliness, a longing for something he couldn't specify? Why did he feel something was eluding him? Now it all became clear.

He had been looking forward to meeting Elimelech again, to having a conversation with him. Elimelech had introduced into his life a new dimension, opening his eyes to an interesting, fascinating world. And now he had disappeared.

"Whatever happened to Elimelech?" Bentzion asked, as if reading his thoughts. "Did he decide to go to a different yeshiva? Maybe he just hasn't been well and will be here soon."

"I also hoped to see him," Aharon sighed. "But I don't think he's coming. He didn't find his place among us. He's searching for something else, a different world."

***

Indeed, Elimelech had enrolled at another *yeshiva gedola*, one that he found increasingly to his liking. He had previously heard many favorable reports about the special personality of the *Mashgiach* at this yeshiva, which convinced him he would find here what he yearned for.

The *Mashgiach*'s first *mussar* talk fulfilled all his expectations and seemed to vindicate his decision to enroll here. The *Mashgiach*'s tone of voice, the form of his talk, reminded Elimelech of Reb Dovid Leib. His face shone with a special, holy light, featuring both firmness and joy without trace of any melancholy or sadness. The *Mashgiach*'s joyous and welcoming approach drew Elimelech close to him right away. Yet his meaningful words penetrated Elimelech's heart, caressing and warming him even as they demanded with high expectations, for they sprang from his natural warmth and love. It was a combination difficult to grasp but surely sensed.

Elimelech had first felt this at that *farbrengen* of Reb Dovid Leib – his simple manner of speech, words coming from the heart, his deep seriousness and thorough honesty, the warmth that caressed but came together with penetrating demands. This *Mashgiach* possessed so many of the same qualities he had first seen in Reb Dovid Leib.

Especially pleasing to Elimelech was how the *Mashgiach* based his words largely on *Tanya* and other works of the great Chassidic masters. To Elimelech this was a sign that the *Mashgiach*'s perspective was correct. He had long decided that wherever there was indifference towards *Chassidus*, he would not find the truth he sought, for he sensed that today it is impossible to achieve spiritual perfection without drawing from Chassidic sources.

The *Mashgiach* opened his talk with with a quote from *Tanya*'s third section, *Iggeres Hateshuva*. The *Baal HaTanya*, he said, explains that many are mistaken in their understanding of the concept of *teshuva* (repentance), thinking it consists of fasting and mortifying one's body, inflicting punishment on oneself.

That is far from the truth. *Teshuva* is primarily one thing alone – a firm decision never to repeat one's foolish errors, never again to transgress the commands of the Divine King, neither by failing to fulfill positive *mitzvos* nor by transgressing His prohibitions. That is the meaning of true *teshuva*: regret for the past and positive resolution for the future. Fasting and self-mortification serve a different purpose, like a gift sent to a king after he has been appeased and has forgiven the act of rebellion, so that the king might again favor the person who caused him displeasure with the same close relationship as had existed before his rebellion. But the appeasement and the *teshuva* itself are accomplished through sincere regret and a firm resolution never to sin again.

The *Mashgiach* expanded on this concept, explaining its practical meaning for yeshiva students: "When Elul starts and an atmosphere of *teshuva* fills the air, some start to confound every area of life, hardly eating or drinking and sleeping erratic hours. And they think that's *teshuva*! Their mistake derives from the *yetzer hara*. By trying to become a sort of holy martyr in an attempt to soothe the suffering *yetzer tov*, they are exchanging what is secondary for what should be most important.

"What are the results of such an approach? After the month of Elul and the *Yamim Nora'im*, the 'Awesome Days' of *Rosh Hashana* and *Yom Kippur*, pass, as we return to our regular routine, everything just reverts to all the negative aspects prevailing last year. That's because the main emphasis wasn't placed on true *teshuva*, which means leaving our sins and resolving to improve in the future, but instead on an utterly secondary aspect – on fasting and self-mortification.

"Therefore," the *Mashgiach* emphasized, "remember this well. Continue your normal routine of eating and sleeping. If you wish, you can reduce physical pleasures a little, but without causing an upheaval in your life. While living life as usual, work to correct what needs correcting. Be careful not to waste time, not to lose focus during Torah study and prayer. Work on improving your *middos* – character traits – and especially the way you actually conduct interpersonal relationships. That's true *teshuva*."

The students' admiration for the *Mashgiach* was evident. They all genuinely loved him. When he spoke, he gazed at them with warmth and affection. His every *mussar* talk injected energy into them, endowing them with new strength to work on their characters. The words, "The *Mashgiach* said...," were part of everyone's conversation. His words were like a higher command, accepted without question.

He inspired the students to study works of *mussar* and *Chassidus*. When Elimelech first saw students studying *Tanya*, *Kesser Shem Tov*, *Noam Elimelech* and other Chassidic works during the *mussar* study session, he could hardly believe his eyes. But he soon realized there were no limitations or preconceived notions here. Everyone studied whatever he felt helped him in serving *Hashem*.

From day to day, Elimelech felt happier for his good fortune to be studying at this yeshiva. He thanked *Hashem* for leading him on the true path. The yeshiva's atmosphere was one of serving *Hashem*, seriously and deeply. The Talmud lectures were excellent, and the students studied diligently. The focus was on thorough understanding and depth, and the Talmud lecturers trained the students never to turn to a new page until they had penetrated the depth of all subjects on the previous one.

The yeshiva's atmosphere reinforced Elimelech's desire, aroused after his conversation with Yonoson, to attend a *Tanya* class at some time. Yonoson had advised him to discuss this with Yisroel, a second year student at his new yeshiva and a prominent regular at the *Tanya* class. Although Elimelech greatly wanted to approach Yisroel, his natural reservation held him back. He wondered how to find a way to talk to him.

It actually happened much sooner than he expected. During one of the *Rosh Yeshiva*'s lectures for the whole yeshiva, he suggested a way to answer the RaAVaD's question on a passage in the RaMBaM's great Halachic code by explaining that, in his opinion, the RaMBaM could be understood differently in such a way that the RaAVaD's question would fall away.

Elimelech was impressed by the *Rosh Yeshiva*'s explanation, which made the RaMBaM seem crystal clear. On first seeing that RaMBaM, he had struggled to understand it, and was happy when he saw the RaAVaD asking the same question. Now, the whole discussion was reversed, and the question instead was why the RaAVaD had not understood the RaMBaM the same way.

Suddenly Yisroel jumped up. If we accept the *Rosh Yeshiva*'s approach to understanding the RaMBaM, he asked, the RaMBaM's words would contradict directly an explicit statement of the *Gemara*! Momentarily, the *Rosh Yeshiva* was taken aback and fell silent, deep in thought.

Elimelech focused on Yisroel's seemingly excellent question. Suddenly he recalled that the ROSh, Rabbeinu Osher, another authoritative *Rishon*, had understood that *Gemara* differently. Quickly he looked up the ROSh at the back of the *Gemara* volume and realized that, indeed, not only did the ROSh understand the *Gemara* differently, but his words seemed to support the RaMBaM's approach.

Delighted with his discovery, Elimelech told Yisroel what the ROSh said. Yisroel remembered that ROSh, but immediately came back with another question. A debate erupted between the two. Elimelech argued that, on the contrary, Yisrael's questions proved that throughout the *Gemara*'s discussion of the subject there are two possible approaches: that of the RaMBaM and the ROSh, on the one hand, and that of the RaAVaD and the RIF on the other!

The *Rosh Yeshiva* complimented Elimelech for his insight and continued his lecture. Yisroel conceded, but only on the surface. His mind was still full of strong questions, and as soon as the lecture was over, he presented them to Elimelech. They sat together dissecting the *Gemara* for a full hour, barely sensing the passage of time.

Eventually, they came to agree with each other, their faces glowing from satisfaction with the clarity of the subject now revealed as a result of their questions and delving into its depth. Their deep discussion created closeness between them which soon led to a general conversation about the yeshiva, the classes, and the *Mashgiach*. All the while, Elimelech tried to steer to what interested him– the *Tanya* class and everything involved with it.

Yisroel seemed not too eager to talk about that subject,

which only strengthened Elimelech's desire to do just that by intentionally returning to the place of *Chassidus* in today's world, and the importance of joy – anything to make Yisroel mention the *Tanya* class.

The subject of joy was what finally brought up the subject. Yisroel told Elimelech an amazing idea he had heard about the month of Elul. When Elul arrives, most people become solemn, even downcast, as they fearfully contemplate the approaching Day of Judgment. Really, however, it should be just the opposite! If every *mitzva* should be fulfilled with joy, as the verse states (*Tehilim*-Psalms 100:2), "Serve *Hashem* with joy," it follows that the *mitzva* of *teshuva*, which is unique among all *mitzvos* in that it rectifies transgressions of all other *mitzvos*, should most certainly be fulfilled with joy!

Therefore, along with the seriousness and the atmosphere of *teshuva* during Elul, there should also be immense joy that we are fortunate to be able to purify ourselves by doing *teshuva*, in preparation for meeting our King on *Rosh Hashana* and *Yom Kippur*.

"From whom did you hear that?" Elimelech suddenly asked.

"From the *Mashpia* who gives the *Tanya* class," Yisroel let the detail slip.

From there, the road was wide open. Elimelech asked Yisroel to let him join the *Tanya* class. "I promise to keep my attendance completely secret!" he assured him.

Yisroel laughed. "You don't have to keep it a secret. It's no shame or sin."

"Do you mean to tell me that you go to the *Tanya* class openly?" Elimelech was shocked.

"I don't understand you," Yisrael replied. "Why not? Here, in our yeshiva, no one is threatening or trying to scare us. Whoever wants can attend the class, on condition that the *Mashpia* giving the class is willing to accept him."

"What do you mean?" Elimelech sounded alarmed. "Does he refuse to accept anyone?"

"Some students come just for the excitement," replied Yisroel "We're not interested in those types. It's a serious class and we want only serious students attending, because otherwise its standard would drop."

"So what does it depend on?" Elimelech asked, holding his breath.

"Mainly on how serious a student is. Whoever sincerely wants to come close to serving *Hashem* and to follow the path of the *Baal HaTanya*, can attend."

"I feel my intentions are serious," said Elimelech, almost pleading.

"Okay," Yisroel agreed. "I'll speak to the *Mashpia* giving the class, and I hope he'll agree to let you join."

A whole week passed without Yisroel telling him yes or no. Elimelech was starting to feel anxious whether Yisroel would give him an answer.

Only on Thursday, after supper, did Yisroel come over to Elimelech and tell him calmly, "At ten o'clock tonight, wait for me in the *beis hamidrash*, and we'll go together to the class. The *Mashpia* wants to meet you."

CHAPTER SEVEN
CHOCHMA, BINA, DAAS

During that evening's study session, Elimelech studied with extra intensity. He felt a need to prepare himself spiritually. He had not expected such a sudden invitation to the *Tanya* class, but the surprise was quickly replaced by a sense of responsibility to refine and purify himself, to make his spiritual side dominant over his material side. He realized they would be discussing profound concepts related to the soul and heart, and that just a clear mind and ready grasp would not be sufficient to absorb them. He would need to elevate himself somewhat out of his ordinary mundane concerns.

His emotions were mixed. On the one hand he was relieved that he would finally be attaining what he had sought for so long. After years of exploring on his own, he would now be entering the gateway that would lead him to his goal. At the same time, however, he realized the need to discipline himself not to get carried away by over-enthusiasm. Attending this class would bring him into a new world, structured and complete in itself from top to bottom. That realization necessitated some degree of self-examination, requiring him to remain cool and level-headed as he listened to the new ideas and tried to absorb them objectively.

As the evening's study session wore on, various thoughts flashed through his mind. Until now, he had always related to *Chassidus* as something straightforward and obvious. Just as there exists *Tanach* – Scripture, the Written Torah – and also the Oral Torah, *Mishna* and Talmud, followed by the *Rishonim* (medieval Torah authorities) and the *Acharonim* (more recent Torah authorities), so are there works of *mussar*, *chakira* (Torah philosophy), and *Chassidus*. Everything had always appeared to him as facets of the single, all-embracing Torah.

Now, however, it occurred to him: What **is** *Chassidus*? What is its essence? What did it come to innovate? Even more pressing on his mind: What is the unique outlook of Chabad *Chassidus*? What is the secret of the special fascination of its foundational work, the *Tanya*? Why are so many fine Jews attracted towards it, while others are afraid to embrace it?

At ten o'clock he accompanied Yisroel to a *shul* on a side street. Fourteen students sat around two tables placed end to end, and Elimelech was the fifteenth. On the way there, Yisroel had explained that Reb Yosef Yitzchak, the *Mashpia* who gave the *Tanya* lesson, did not like teaching large classes, preferring small, quiet groups of less participants, which allowed a feeling of closeness and rapport to develop between him and his students and among themselves. Once a class filled up and enough students were interested, a new group could form. This class, Yisrael said, was already full.

From where he sat, Elimelech scanned the faces of the other participants. Some he recognized from his yeshiva, among them older students from higher classes. The rest, whom he did not know, were presumably from other yeshivos.

What impressed Elimelech first of all was the general sense of seriousness. The faces of all participants showed that they approached this study with gravity. There was not the slightest sense of frivolity, no laid back attitude of taking it easy, as is normally characteristic of teenagers. Everyone evidently sensed the purpose for which they had gathered here.

Reb Yosef Yitzchak was a young man, probably in his mid-twenties. A wide, black beard adorned his face, and his deep, brown eyes were penetrating. Even when he made a joking remark or smiled, his characteristic seriousness never left him. Elimelech noticed later that, once the class was over, it was as if a burden rolled off the *Mashpia*'s shoulders, and he became more relaxed and open. Clearly his duty to teach *Tanya* to these young students and to guide them in serving *Hashem* imposed on him a heavy sense of responsibility.

Elimelech looked into the *Tanya* text in front of him. How incredible, he thought, how such a small book has changed the lives of so many. On their way to the class, Yisroel had mentioned that when the renowned Rabbi Levi Yitzchak, the *Rav* of Berditchev, had received the *Tanya* after its first publication in Kislev, 5557 (1796) and had a chance to study it, he had exclaimed, "How did the author manage to fit such a great G-d into such a small book?" The special atmosphere of seriousness in the room gave that story a whole new meaning.

The class was currently studying Chapter 4 of the first section of *Tanya*. For the sake of the new student, apparently, Reb Yosef Yitzchak summarized the main points of the previous chapters. He spoke calmly, in a pleasant tone, and with great clarity.

"In these chapters, the Alter Rebbe explains the structure of the Jewish soul. In Chapter 1 he explained that, within every Jew, two souls are functioning – a Divine soul and an animal soul.

In the same chapter he explains the essential character of the animal soul. In the second chapter, he explains the essence of the Divine soul which is within every one of us.

"The animal soul gives life to the body. It's also the source of all negative character traits, such as anger, pride, lust for material pleasures, frivolity, laziness and sadness.

"In contrast, every Jew has a second soul, the Divine soul, which is 'literally part of G-d from Above.' There's no difference in this between souls of saintly *tzadikim* and those of simple Jews: all originate from the Divine thought and wisdom, and *Hashem* and His wisdom are a single entity.

"So there you have the essence of the two souls.

"Each soul also has powers. In Chapter 3, we learned about the Divine soul's powers: The three intellectual powers are *chochma* (wisdom), *bina* (understanding), and *daas* (awareness), referred to by the acronym '*ChaBaD*,' which enable us to reflect upon G-dliness. This reflection produces the seven powers of emotion: *chessed* (kindness), expressed in love of *Hashem*, *gevura* (severity), expressed in awe of *Hashem*, *tiferes* (beauty), etc.

"Now, in Chapter 4, the Alter Rebbe explains that the soul and its powers also have what he calls 'garments.' These are the three media by which each of the two souls expresses itself – thought, speech, and action. 'Thought' here does not refer to the mind's understanding of a concept, for that understanding is accomplished through the intellectual powers of *ChaBaD*. 'Thought,' on the other hand, is the expression of the mind, the actual process of thinking about anything, whether intellectual or emotional, and it's expressed in the words and letters of one's language.

"Thus, thought, speech and action are not part of the soul and its powers, but are merely modes of expression through which the soul reveals what it wants to reveal. When a person understands or feels something, he thinks about it, speaks about it, or acts according to the implications of what he has understood or felt. That's why thought, speech and action are called 'garments' of the soul, because they're each like a garment in which the intellectual or emotional content can be clothed."

As Elimelech listened, he felt a wave of warm pleasure filling his being. The way Reb Yosef Yitzchak developed these subtle, delicate concepts about the human soul gave him a wonderful sense of clarity. Everything was so clear and immediately understandable that, when Reb Yosef Yitzchak spoke, Elimelech almost felt he could actually see the concepts before his eyes. Everything was described in such vibrant and vivid form. Never had he encountered such broad and profound explanation of concepts that are so refined and abstract. Yes, he had seen the terms *chochma, bina, daas,* which obviously refer to intellect, and he knew these were higher than *chessed, gevura, tiferes,* the first three of the seven emotions. But, in his mind, these terms had always been mere symbols for abstract, undefined concepts, somewhere in the higher spiritual worlds, beyond the grasp of the human mind. It had never occurred to him that these concepts were related to the human soul, too.

He had always regarded the soul as a single, indivisible entity. Like all other yeshiva students, he knew about the existence of the *yetzer tov* and the *yetzer hara* and the constant struggle between them. Everything had been evenly split between black and white. Now he felt like a color-blind person who suddenly begins to see the wonderful world around him in its full array of colors and sub-hues. He began to realize the soul's great complexity and the wide range of powers that exist and function within it. Now he realized how the soul had many layers through which everything passes until it descends to the point where it becomes expressed within the person and the world around him.

"The term 'garments' has two meanings," Reb Yosef Yitzchak continued. "On the one hand, the term illustrates that thought, speech and action are not part of the person himself; they're like a garment he wears. By definition, a garment is distinct from its wearer. On the other hand, it has a special connection to its wearer. It's not an ornament placed on him without any need to fit him. A garment has to fit the wearer well. This aspect is true also in one's thought, speech, and action.

"Now let's understand these two aspects. The first aspect of garments expresses how they are distinct from the person. It's easy to perceive how there is no need for any connection to exist between the person's essence and his garments, between what he actually is and what he thinks, speaks or does.

"Let's take a simple example. A person can write 2+2, and then record the total as 5. Just as he can write it (action), he can also say it (speech), and can even imagine it (thought)! Obviously, there need be no connection between the 'garments' and the person himself."

"But that's just foolish," one of the boys interjected, trying to make sense of the *Mashpia*'s words. "Anyone who writes, says or thinks that knows it's impossible and makes no sense."

"True, that's exactly what I meant," Reb Yosef Yitzchak

explained. "He himself knows it's foolish, yet that doesn't stop him from writing, speaking, and thinking it. In this way we sense the distance of a person's 'garments' from his identity. Although we expect the 'garments' to express the logic of one's intellectual abilities, in reality they may express the absolute opposite of what the intellect understands to be true, even to the extent of total absurdity."

"But if he can think that 2+2=5," the same student continued to argue, "then even the intellect is not compelled to convey real understanding."

"No, pay attention to what you have just said," Reb Yosef Yitzchak answered. "He can think it, yes. But he will never understand it. His brain will never grasp or accept that 2+2=5. Such a thing is only possible at the level of the 'garments.'"

"Let's use an example from the level of emotions," Reb Yosef Yitzchak continued. "Imagine someone who hates another person fiercely. He can still act towards him kindly, speak to him nicely, even using terms of endearment, and even force himself to think lovingly about him. There's a huge difference between what he feels in his heart and what he does, speaks or thinks, but it's still completely possible for the two opposites to coexist."

"But such behavior is insincere. It's merely an artificial façade," pointed out the student on Elimelech's right.

Elimelech observed him carefully. He looked young, maybe about his own age. But the intense seriousness he expressed was like an adult's.

"We'll address that soon," Reb Yosef Yitzchak answered

encouragingly. "For now, we're not discussing whether or not the behavior is sincere. Important is the fact that these 'garments' are totally separate from a person's essential character, to the extent that it's possible for the 'garments' to express the opposite of the true content of one's intellect and emotions.

"Let's demonstrate this in a clearer way," Reb Yosef Yitzchak continued his breakdown of the concept. "It's easy to understand why we say the powers of the soul – intellect and emotions – are part of the person himself, while the 'garments' are external to him.

"When we see a great Torah scholar, with deep knowledge of *Shas* (the entire Talmud), and of the *Poskim*, the great Torah authorities of later eras, and also a deep understanding of the Creator's greatness, a man of great wisdom and brilliant intellect, we consider him to be an exalted personality, at least in the area of intellect. He's clearly different from an ignoramus, and there's no comparison between them.

"Regarding emotions, the difference is even more intense: The exalted personality's heart burns with a strong love for *Hashem*, his soul longs and yearns for its Creator. For him, all worldly pleasures are worthless, for he thirsts for G-dliness, and is utterly overawed by *Hashem*'s sovereignty, trembling at the thought of being separated from Him for even a moment. Such a personality is unique, for he elevates his essence to such a high level of holiness and spirituality. You won't find such individuals easily; such a level is reached only after long years of intense toil of heart and soul.

"But all this refers to intellect and emotions. When we refer to the person's 'garments,' however, the picture is entirely different. From the point of view of the 'garments,' it's very possible that the exalted personality and the simple ignoramus can appear identical. It's possible for a simple, unrefined Jew to get up one morning and decide to sit in the *beis hamidrash* and study diligently all day. Despite his previous coarseness and total immersion in physical desires, he can suddenly decide to abstain from it all and devote himself entirely to holiness, Torah and *mitzvos*."

"If that's the case," one of the participants asked, "wouldn't such behavior be a sign he's changed?"

"Not necessarily," Reb Yosef Yitzchak answered. "He might be acting that way just for fun, or just trying to prove to his friends that he, too, can be a *tzaddik*!"

"If that's his motivation," the same student commented, "then such behavior wouldn't last very long."

"Practically speaking, you're right," Reb Yosef Yitzchak agreed. "Only when someone acts that way consistently, over a long period of time, does he prove he has indeed changed. But that's not the point we're trying to make. Theoretically, it **is** possible for someone to act that way for 120 years, in total contrast to his inner character. He can remain essentially coarse, continuing to crave all worldly pleasures, yet force himself never to fulfill those desires.

"All of this proves to us," Reb Yosef Yitzchak concluded, "just how foreign the 'garments' are to one's identity. They're exactly like his physical clothing: When he wants, he puts it on, and when he changes his mind, he takes it off. Just as a royal robe doesn't prove the wearer is the king, so are the 'garments' of one's soul – thought, speech, and action – not part of his essence and they can't prove for certain who he is on the inside."

"But thought, speech, and action like those are not authentic," objected the student to Elimelech's right. "They haven't been perfected."

"Okay, now we've reached the next point," Reb Yosef Yitzchak smiled, "the very idea I was about to express. As I explained before, this aspect of the 'garments' is only one of their qualities. There's another aspect, expressed in the fact that a garment needs to fit the person.

"The examples I've given until now describe 'garments' that are imperfect and inauthentic. Those examples are unusual, because people don't generally behave that way. An authentic, perfect garment must, above all, fit the person and match his essence. Usually, people speak and think according to what they understand in their mind and feel in their heart, not the opposite.

"That's why, when we talk about perfect, authentic 'garments,' we're referring to thought, speech, and action that correctly express one's identity, 'garments' that match his inner character.

"But this quality alone still doesn't justify calling them 'garment.' Such a state exists in any system of cause and effect where the result matches the cause. It doesn't truly express the full implications of the Alter Rebbe's choice of referring to these functions as 'garments.'

"The term 'garments' implies much more: When a person

speaks, for example, what he understands in his mind, it doesn't mean he's merely speaking words that match his understanding (as in a cause and effect relationship), but much more. His words are a garment in which his intellect and understanding are clothed.

"The same is true of his emotions. When one utters words of love and affection, they aren't only a result of what he feels in his heart. The love is clothed in the words and expressed through them. The words of love are like a garment that allows the love to burst forth from within and to find expression. The love in his heart is discovered by being clothed in his words of affection."

"Is there some way to understand this better?" asked one of the students.

"Certainly," Reb Yosef Yitzchak replied. "Sometimes we can sense this enclothment very vividly. For example, you can sense it in anyone's tone of voice. When talking of matters important to him, his tone of voice changes and you can sense in his voice how important the topic is to him. When speaking words of affection, you can feel how his inner love is transmitted through his words. Even from his actions you can sense this, albeit more subtly. When one does some act out of a deep soul bond with another, it can be sensed how his inner warmth is invested in that act and that it isn't being performed just superficially. This is how the soul's powers are clothed in the 'garments.'

"This is the real explanation of the term 'garments,' when we refer to thought, speech, and action," Reb Yosef Yitzchak concluded the class. "Remember to keep these two aspects in mind. It'll be important throughout the rest of the chapter, as well as in the coming chapters, when we discuss the superior quality of the 'garments' and the elevation they bring to the soul."

The *Tanya* class was over, but the participants begged Reb Yosef Yitzchak to tell them something about the special *avoda* of Elul and *Rosh Hashana* according to *Chassidus*. Reb Yosef Yitzchak agreed and for some time elaborated on the deeper meaning of *teshuva*, as based on the verse, "And the spirit shall return to *Hashem* who gave it." He also spoke about the meaning of *shofar* blowing as explained in *Chassidus*, about the spiritual service of crowning the Divine King on *Rosh Hashana*, and much more.

Elimelech sat spellbound. His eyes were fixed on the *Mashpia*, and his ears absorbed every word. He could not properly digest or reflect on what he saw and heard, for he was completely captivated by the shining light flowing through him in that lesson.

Walking back to the yeshiva, his legs carried him of their own accord as his mind remained immersed in that evening's experiences. In his best dreams he could never have imagined it was possible to study and analyze such subtle, abstract concepts with such breadth and clarity, in the same way one analyzed the reasoning of a law in the RaMBaM. The revelation overwhelmed him.

But what he discovered in that first class was just a tip of the iceberg. New surprises, no less amazing, awaited him as he discovered in the coming weeks.

CHAPTER EIGHT
WHAT IS *CHASSIDUS?*

That year, the *Yamim Nora'im* of *Rosh Hashana* and *Yom Kippur* exceeded anything Elimelech had ever experienced. His prayers were different, more sincere and heartfelt, and often he had the feeling it was the first time he was authentically experiencing these Days of Judgment. A sense of freshness, renewal and depth enveloped him.

The impact on him of the few *Tanya* classes he had already attended was immense. Every class opened a new window to change his worldview, deepening how he related to the world around him, clarifying everything. The world of *Chassidus* that had opened and spread out before him began to captivate his entire being. It was a mighty power that seemed to draw him further inward into *Chassidus*. At the end of the latest class, as the participants sat and talked with Reb Yosef Yitzchak, he had turned to Elimelech with a smile, "With you my work is very simple; it's clear you were born with a *Chassidishe* soul...!"

Indeed, the more he penetrated deeper into the world of *Chassidus*, the more he felt he had found his place, that these concepts were fundamentally connected with him. When he thought deeply about it, he realized something most interesting, that even before he had been privileged to get to know about *Chassidus*, he had discovered Chassidic tendencies within himself on his own. Now he realized that, even earlier in his life, his behavior and thought patterns had revealed approaches remarkably similar to those of the path of *Chassidus*. This enabled his integration into the world of *Chassidus* to develop naturally and effortlessly.

When he tried to define these thoughts in precise terms, however, he was unsuccessful. His desire to clarify for himself the distinctions between the world of *Chassidus* and everything outside it left him baffled. Within himself he sensed the difference clearly, but as soon as he tried to define and express it in words that could be shared with others, he felt it didn't work, that his heart's feelings could not be expressed in words.

That's why he avoided discussing the topic with his new friends at yeshiva. It was common knowledge he had joined the *Tanya* classes, and they often tried to hear what he had to say about it. But he always preferred to turn the conversation elsewhere and not to answer their questions.

He felt a need to internalize everything really well before it would make sense to discuss it with others. His *chavrusa*, his study partner, tried repeatedly to raise the subject again and again. But Elimelech would just smile and keep quiet. His partner had no choice but to let it go, although he did regard him as somewhat strange.

Rosh Hashana and *Yom Kippur* gave Elimelech much food for thought. They were like the end of a rope he could grasp as he struggled to define what *Chassidus* essentially is. The Chassidic approach to these holy days, as gained from the conversations with Reb Yosef Yitzchak, had enough substance to point him toward the overall perspective of *Chassidus* on everything.

In previous years his emotions and the tone of his prayers during the *Yamim Nora'im* had been permeated with fear and awe.

The overall feeling had been one of tension, even terror. *Rosh Hashana* was the Day of Judgment, and *Yom Kippur* was when the decree for the entire creation was determined – a terrifying concept that aroused him to pray from deep in his heart, for his life seemed to hang in the balance.

This year, though, he experienced a whole new dimension that inspired and uplifted him. The concept of *Rosh Hashana* as the day of the coronation of the Divine King, of establishing and accepting His kingship, provided new depth and meaning. That *Rosh Hashana* is the Day of Judgment became just one detail within the much larger picture of the renewal of the entire physical and spiritual universe that takes place on the first day of the new year.

The Chassidic explanation of *Yom Kippur*, too, gave the day a whole new meaning. On that day, the Jewish people's essential connection to *Hashem* is revealed, to the point that "the Jewish people are alone with their King," and the soul's innermost core, its "*yechida*," becomes revealed as united with the *Yochid*, the one single G-d.

These Chassidic insights enriched his sense of awe of *Hashem* with a thirst and yearning to become close to Him, a deep feeling accompanied by joy and upliftment. For the first time ever, he was able to feel the seemingly contradictory sensations of "rejoicing while trembling" (*Tehilim*-Psalms 2:11), realizing how both the rejoicing and the trembling derive from the same basic point.

All this prompted him to pray very devoutly on these days. As he reflected on the meaning of the prayers in the *machzor* (holiday prayer book) of the *Yamim Nora'im*, he began to see how perfectly they corresponded to the Chassidic explanations Reb Yosef Yitzchak had taught. This fact changed his whole focus of prayer in general. It was no longer just begging for mercy, but also, and primarily, the act of crowning *Hashem* as Sovereign of the universe.

This new direction broadened his entire perspective, arousing a sense of exaltation. This point, he felt, could enable him to define the overall essence of *Chassidus*. After the *Yamim Nora'im*, he tried to clarify it for himself. Deep within him, he sensed it very clearly: *Chassidus*, he reasoned within himself, is the Torah's inner dimension, so it must reveal the inner layers and depth of everything. Therefore, as soon as *Chassidus* shines its light on anything, that concept or entity receives depth, a more profound perspective. Even if that concept or entity may at first seem clear and well understood, it receives infinite new depth after the light of *Chassidus* shines upon it. It is as if *Chassidus* opens a window to the infinite nature of everything, to its essential loftiness that is ultimately beyond comprehension.

That must be why joy is so characteristic of *Chassidus*, he continued thinking, why happiness so permeates the Chassidic world. When everything acquires such inner meaning and depth, it inevitably brings feelings of joy. When one feels so clearly the importance of every most minor detail and the privilege of fulfilling *Hashem*'s will by utilizing it to serve Him, one must become happy and full of vitality.

Nevertheless, Elimelech still sensed he was just touching the outer edges of *Chassidus*, grasping only its externality. What, essentially, is *Chassidus*? Is it identical with *Kabbala*, which also explains the *sod*, the mystical secrets and inner dimension of everything? Yet the way of life and world view of those involved in *Kabbala* are clearly not the same as those involved in *Chassidus*. So *Chassidus* isn't *Kabbala*.

These thoughts continued to bother Elimelech: What, essentially, is *Chassidus*?

***

At the end of the next *Tanya* class, Elimelech threw out this question that so bothered him: "What is *Chassidus*?"

The question piqued the other students' curiosity. They, too, were interested to know.

Reb Yosef Yitzchak tried to minimize the question. "Here, we're studying *Chassidus*. This is it!"

"Yes, we're studying *Chassidus*, but we don't know what it actually is," Elimelech pressed.

"What is it? Why, it's *Chassidus*!" the *Mashpia* smiled. The students smiled, too, but fixed their eyes on him, awaiting his answer and a satisfying explanation for this excellent question.

Elimelech had thought too long and hard about the question to be satisfied with a superficial answer. He persisted, "We know the Torah consists of four layers of depth, which we refer to as 'PaRDeS' – *p'shat, remez, drush, sod*. When we study *Chumash* with *Rashi*'s commentary, we know that's *p'shat*, the simple, straightforward meaning. When one studies *Kabbala*, he knows it's *sod*, the mystical meaning. But when we study *Chassidus*, what are we studying? Is it *sod*? Or is *Chassidus* perhaps a fifth Torah dimension?"

"Perhaps you should try to answer the question on your own," Reb Yosef Yitzchak encouraged, turning it over to the students.

For a moment, all was quiet. Elimelech glanced around the room, watching his friends' faces as they thought about it. For a moment, he considered sharing the ideas that had occurred to him until then. But he decided to keep quiet and hear what the others had to say.

"When we think about it," one of the students said, "it's interesting that *Chassidus* seems to include all the levels of *PaRDeS*. In the *Chassidus* we've learned so far, we find new interpretations of verses from the *Tanach* that sound like *p'shat,* and others that follow the method of *drush* (non-literal interpretation). We've also encountered several *gematriyos* (numerical values of Hebrew words) and allusions hidden in the Torah's words, which are from the level called *remez*; and many, many explanations based on *Kabbala*, the level of *sod*."

"It's true that *Chassidus* includes some instances of *p'shat, drush*, and *remez*," another student argued. "But *sod* is the predominant part of *Chassidus*, to an extent much greater than the other levels of *PaRDeS*. Since the goal of *Chassidus* is to explain the inner meaning of everything, that is more connected to the level of *sod* than to any of the other three."

"So you're saying that *Chassidus* is *Kabbala*?" a third student challenged. "So what then was the Baal Shem Tov's innovation? After all, *Kabbala* has always been part of the Torah!"

"That's true," the second student responded, explaining his position. "*Chassidus* is *Kabbala*, and the Baal Shem Tov spread it to the wider Jewish community, in contrast to previous generations when only a few holy individuals studied it."

"According to what you're saying," a fourth student joined the fray, "the Baal Shem Tov's innovation seems to be just a technicality. He taught nothing new but just decided to reveal what was previously known only to a select, elite few. But it's well-known that the Baal Shem Tov revealed a new bright light and a new way of serving *Hashem*!"

Another student offered a compromise: "*Chassidus* is very similar to *Kabbala*, but it's not just *Kabbala*. It's *Kabbala* clothed in human understanding. *Chassidus* explains *Kabbala* and transforms it into Torah that we can grasp, just like *Nigleh* – the Torah as it's revealed in the Talmud and *Halacha*."

The first student reemphasized his original point: "Nevertheless, as I said before, we all see that *Chassidus* deals not only with *sod*, the mystical level of the Torah, but also includes so many interpretations on the other levels of *p'shat, remez*, and *drush*!"

"That's because all parts of the Torah are interconnected," the second student countered. "In *kedusha*, the holiness deriving from *Hashem*, there is an interconnection between all its aspects, which is why the level of *sod* includes interpretations from all other aspects of the Torah."

Finally, silence prevailed. Reb Yosef Yitzchak was gazing at some vague point across the room, deep in thought. The students looked towards him, waiting for him to speak. But he gave no sign of any intention to speak. He seemed to be expecting the students to delve deeper...

Elimelech, too, felt that his fellow students' answers were not at all satisfying. They all seemed too superficial. *Chassidus*, he felt, was much more than an explanation of *Kabbala*.

"According to what you've all been saying," Elimelech summarized, "*Chassidus* seems to be no more than a commentary on *Kabbala*. Can we really accept that this is the essence of *Chassidus*, and that's all? Could a mere explanation of *Kabbala* bring about the tremendous revolution that *Chassidus* achieved? Could it have provoked such sharp opposition as resulted from the appearance of *Chassidus*? *Chassidus* wrought a revolutionary innovation, bringing an utterly new light into the Jewish world."

"It's true, that's the way it seems to be," the boy on Elimelech's right agreed. "So we must say *Chassidus* is a new revelation of the Torah, beyond the other four Torah levels of *PaRDeS*."

"How can you say that?" several students vehemently objected at once. "Everyone knows there are only four Torah levels, not five!"

"That's right," said a student who had been in this class longer than all of them, but had not yet participated in the debate. "In the Rebbe's *sichos* (Torah talks), he always shows sources in the *Gemara*, *Kabbala* and other authoritative works for every idea in *Chassidus*, emphasizing that even the most innovative insights of *Chassidus* all have sources in Torah works from before the appearance of *Chassidus*. So how can *Chassidus* be a new, fifth Torah aspect?"

"So, what then **is** *Chassidus*?" Elimelech repeated his original question, which this time sounded much deeper and more difficult to answer.

Finally, Reb Yosef Yitzchak joined the discussion.

"*Chassidus* is *P'nimius HaTorah*, the inner dimension of Torah," he said softly.

"You mean it's *Kabbala*?" several students asked together.

"No, *Kabbala* is the *sod* of the Torah," the *Mashpia* answered.

"So what is *Chassidus*?" the students wondered.

"*Chassidus* is the inner dimension of the Torah," the *Mashpia* repeated. "It's the inner dimension of *p'shat*, of *remez*, of *drush*, and of *sod*. It's the inner dimension of the entire Torah."

The room fell silent. The students had no idea how to digest the *Mashpia*'s words. What is the meaning of "the inner dimension of everything"? They stared at him, expecting his explanation.

"Let's address this from another angle," he began to explain. "We've often mentioned the *Moshiach*'s reply to the Baal Shem Tov's question, 'When will you come?' He told him, 'When your wellsprings will be spread outwards.' We've also explained that the connection between the ultimate *Geula* (Redemption) and the dissemination of the 'wellsprings' of *Chassidus* is that the teachings of *Chassidus* are a preparation for the *Geula*, because they're a 'taste' of what will be revealed following that *Geula*.

"What will be revealed in that future era? Surely we're already learning Torah now. So what will be the Torah of *Moshiach*, compared to which, our Sages say, the Torah we study now will be like nonsense?

"The answer is that now we're studying only the Torah's external aspect, its 'body,' so to speak, for it involves how to observe it in the material world. But *Moshiach* will reveal its inner dimension, the Torah's 'soul,' as the holy *Zohar* calls it. Revealed in the future will be the essence of the Torah. *Chassidus* is a taste, a sample, of what will be revealed when *Moshiach* comes. It is a radiance of the same light that *Moshiach* will cause to shine."

"But what is that inner dimension?" asked Elimelech.

"That I can't answer," Reb Yosef Yitzchak said. "Some concepts defy description of their essence. Just as we cannot speak about the essence of *Hashem*, so can't we define the essence of the Torah, which is His wisdom. It's just like the impossibility of defining a person's essential, inner life-force, his soul. None of these are at all within our grasp."

"But we do study *Chassidus* and understand it," one of the students pointed out.

"Indeed, we can study it and sense its light. But we can't define it," Reb Yosef Yitzchak clarified. "Studying and understanding it is possible. But to define its essential nature is impossible."

"We don't understand!" most of the students chimed in.

"Okay, I see we've explained too soon what should come later," Reb Yosef Yitzchak backtracked. "If you'd be patient and study more *Chassidus*, you'd understand this more easily. But I'll give you an analogy to make it easier to grasp. Do you feel the soul inside you?"

"Of course," one student answered, as the others nodded in agreement. "Our every movement, sensation or thought expresses the soul within us."

"Okay," Reb Yosef Yitzchak acknowledged. "But what is the soul you all feel? Is it intellect, or emotion, or desire? Is it a hand, head or heart? What is the soul?"

"It's a spiritual entity higher than all the limbs and senses," they answered.

"Yes, but what is it?" Reb Yosef Yitzchak persisted.

The silence now filling the room confirmed that the students understood what he meant. Now he proceeded to present the other side.

"Now please tell me, what is intellect if not the soul as clothed within intellect? What is emotion if not the soul as clothed within emotion? What is action if not the soul coming down to that level to make things happen? Are all these something other than the soul?"

"No, of course it's the soul," the students agreed. "The soul is expressed in a person's every movement."

"Now, pay attention!" Reb Yosef Yitzchak concluded. "On the one hand, you agree it's impossible to define the soul's essential nature and we're incapable of saying what it actually is. On the other hand, it's everything: desire, intellect, emotion, action, a person's every movement.

"The same is true of *Chassidus*. Its essential nature is beyond definition and cannot be comprehended at all. It's absolutely abstract, beyond the bounds of understanding and intellect. But along with that, it's expressed in everything, in *p'shat*, in *remez*, in *drush*, and in *sod*. It includes everything, but its essence is exalted above everything. It's the inner dimension.

"In regard to the 'body' of the Torah, *Nigleh*, the Torah's revealed aspect, *Chassidus* added nothing. Therefore every concept in *Chassidus* must have a source in the Talmud, *Kabbala*, etc., as one of you mentioned earlier. Nevertheless, *Chassidus* introduced a spirit of newness into everything, breathing new vitality and soul into every Torah subject. Anything studied in the light of *Chassidus* is transformed, becoming bright and alive.

"All this is apparent not only in the Torah, but also in people. From a physical perspective, perhaps there's no difference between a *Chassid*'s Torah study and *mitzva* observance and those of someone not yet privileged to experience the light of *Chassidus*. Both study Torah and observe *mitzvos* (although *Chassidus* does lead to more *hiddur mitzva* – doing it in the best possible way, with extra care for every detail). But in regard to the soul, the difference is from one extreme to the other. The *Chassid* is alive, full of joy, as he and the *mitzva* become one, just as a soul is one with the body."

With that Reb Yosef Yitzchak concluded his remarkable explanation.

CHAPTER NINE

INTERNAL AND EXTERNAL

One evening Elimelech was summoned for a private meeting with the *Mashgiach*. Ever since he had started the new yeshiva year, two months earlier, he had been expecting this. He was surprised it had taken so long, but was happy for the opportunity to meet personally with this outstanding personality who so deeply impressed all the students.

They loved these conversations with him and, when summoned, went happily even if they expected his rebuke for some personal fault. Even when he had no choice but to speak sternly, students felt how much he loved them, for he always found a way to soften his words, often with humor.

Since entering the yeshiva, Elimelech had tried to uncover the story of the *Mashgiach*'s background, the yeshiva where he had studied, his Torah teachers, and how he had become the yeshiva's *Mashgiach*. But it was evident that the *Mashgiach* did not talk much about his own background and was especially reluctant to share personal details of his life. The secrecy just increased Elimelech's curiosity to find out. He tried indirectly to elicit information from the Talmud lecturers and senior students, but beyond generalities was unsuccessful.

He did learn that the *Mashgiach* had studied for some time in Radin, at the yeshiva of the renowned *Chafetz Chayim*, before proceeding to other yeshivos. As a refugee in the Soviet Union during World War II, he had lived among Chassidim and was attracted towards *Chassidus*. After immigrating to Israel following the war, he would dedicate every available hour to Torah study, while eking out a meager living from odd jobs.

Several years later, when this yeshiva's founder recalled the refined young scholar he had met during the war, he searched for his whereabouts and came to beg him to become the *Rosh Yeshiva*. But he was met with adamant refusal. After the founder persisted, he eventually agreed to serve not as *Rosh Yeshiva* but as *Mashgiach*. Despite this, the *Mashgiach* was considered to be the yeshiva's most influential faculty member.

From the *Mashgiach*'s talks to the entire yeshiva body, Elimelech concluded that what had made the strongest impression on him was the self-sacrifice of Chassidim for keeping *Yiddishkeit* alive even under the most difficult circumstances. Often he described the greatness of *mesiras nefesh*, utter self-sacrifice, and the need to serve *Hashem* with such devotion even today when we are not compelled literally to give up our lives. The need to devote one's will, physical life and possessions, together with one's spiritual life and attainments, to *Hashem* remains forever relevant, he would emphasize. Where there is self-sacrifice, he would say, that is a place of truth.

Elimelech especially admired the *Mashgiach*'s unpretentiousness, a simple humility that was authentic and natural. It was a true humility that showed how he truly considered himself an ordinary person, undeserving of special attention. Sometimes he passed among the students during their morning prayers, and would even fix someone's *tefilin* straps that had become twisted, doing it with utter simplicity as if this was his classmate!

With some measure of awe but also with inner joy, Elimelech approached the *Mashgiach*'s study. At the door, he hesitated for a moment, starting to get excited.But he composed himself and entered. Behind his desk, the *Mashgiach* awaited him with a broad, heartfelt smile.

***

"What do you study during the *mussar* study session?" was the *Mashgiach*'s opening question.

"I study *Mesilas Yeshorim, Reishis Chochma*, and some *Tanya*," Elimelech replied.

The *Mashgiach* was interested in what exactly he studied in those works, and he probed, pleasantly and calmly. Elimelech responded to all his questions while, at the back of his mind, wondering what was the *Mashgiach*'s purpose for asking it all. The conversation was very friendly. From time to time, the *Mashgiach* elaborated on points Elimelech mentioned.

Suddenly he asked, "Do you understand what you're studying in *Tanya*?"

Elimelech was bewildered. For a moment he hesitated whether to tell the *Mashgiach* about his participation in the *Tanya* class? But immediately he decided there was no reason to hide it.

"On my own, I didn't understand the depth, but I started attending an extracurricular *Tanya* class, and the *Mashpia* there explains everything very well," Elimelech replied.

The *Mashgiach* fixed him with a penetrating gaze, and Elimelech lowered his eyes. He felt the *Mashgiach* was still focused on him, so he didn't dare to look up. For a long while he sat that way, full of trepidation at the *Mashgiach*'s reaction.

Finally the *Mashgiach* asked, "What brought you to the *Tanya* class?"

Elimelech felt his self-confidence evaporating. He had no idea how to start telling the *Mashgiach* about the many difficult questions that had bothered him, about his insatiable yearning that had drawn him to the class.

"I was searching... I wanted to find the proper way to serve *Hashem*. *Tanya* seemed to me to be the right and true way..." Elimelech stumbled over his words.

The *Mashgiach* continued to probe, as his face became more and more serious. Elimelech did not know how to interpret this, but decided not to hide anything from him, and proceeded to share the whole saga of his questions and searches.

When he finished telling everything he had been through, the *Mashgiach* rested his head on his hands, his eyes almost closed, for several minutes. Elimelech was terrified, feeling like a defendant awaiting his verdict. Would the *Mashgiach* forbid him from going to the *Tanya* class or would he encourage him to continue?

The *Mashgiach* raised his head, and started speaking quietly, almost to himself. "*Chassidus* emphasizes that the *yetzer hara* knows how to wear a 'silk *kapota*.' He doesn't always appear as a lustful character, trying to entice one to sin. Sometimes he plays the role of an enthusiastic *Chassid*, urging one to pore through holy books, to take on all kinds of Chassidic conduct, to act piously and as an ascetic. Yet it's the same *yetzer hara* who wants to ensnare one to fall into worldly desires and various prohibitions.

"When he finds a serious young man who wants with all his heart to come close to *Hashem* and to serve Him, the *yetzer hara* knows very well he won't get to trap him in his net by suggesting he not study properly, not pray devoutly, or not avoid what's prohibited, for then the young man will realize immediately with whom he's dealing and will flee from him as from fire.

"So what does the *yetzer hara* do? He changes his mask, masquerading as G-d-fearing, as one who seeks spirituality and yearns for *Hashem*. With such a mask he tricks the young man into righteous conduct that is beyond his level. The young man starts acting like a devout *Chassid*, studying subjects that attract him with their mystery and mystique, while in reality he doesn't understand them. As a result, he soon becomes an empty vessel plastered with a shining veneer.

"This superficiality makes him rotten inside. He'll be unable to attain anything in any fundamental way, with any deep soul connection. His entire being becomes imprisoned in the superficiality of everything, and he's living a lie...

"Instead of praying devoutly, with due seriousness, his prayer becomes a show – for himself and others. He'll wave his hands, roll his eyes heavenward, and tighten his forehead in false concentration, while swaying back and forth. He becomes a slave to all kinds of vague emotions, and thinks this is the meaning of prayer to *Hashem*."

The *Mashgiach* fell silent, deep in thought. Elimelech still didn't understand what he was getting at, but his last point, about prayer, found an echo in him. For some time, he had carefully watched how the *Mashgiach* prayed in a unique manner. No external movement was apparent, his hands never moved and his body never shook from side to side. Only occasionally did he make slight movements of the head and body but never more than that. He just prayed quietly with virtually no movement.

Now the *Mashgiach* continued talking again. "When a hand is raised up during prayer, it should happen only if it is utterly spontaneous. But if someone feels himself raising his hand or rolling his eyes, that's superficial. Such behavior encourages falsehood. Chassidim always ran away from superficiality as from fire. If any Chassidim ever did make such motions, it was because they were so deeply absorbed in their prayer that they didn't even realize they were moving.

"Pay attention now to what I'm saying," the *Mashgiach*'s gaze bore into Elimelech. "Reflect carefully on the feelings that draw you towards *Chassidus*. Check whether they are honest and authentic, or whether perhaps you're attracted only by the externalities."

***

Elimelech left the *Mashgiach*'s room confused and perplexed. He still could not grasp what the *Mashgiach* was getting at. Did he want him to stop attending *Tanya* classes? Was he unhappy he was learning *Chassidus*? If so, why didn't he just tell him that straight out?

On second thought, he didn't think the *Mashgiach* wanted to cut him off from *Chassidus*. The more he thought about it, the more it seemed that the *Mashgiach* was trying to get Elimelech to ensure that his connection with *Chassidus* become more authentic and internalized. It seemed, Elimelech mused, that the *Mashgiach* believed his involvement with *Chassidus* might derive from a sense of adventurousness within him, which he was trying to prevent.

But then how could he differentiate between true inner longing to serve *Hashem* as *Chassidus* teaches and curiosity for the mysterious? He believed his intentions to be true and internally motivated, but maybe it was just his imagination. How can one measure whether something is true or false, internal or superficial?

These thoughts bothered him no end. The longer he considered it, his frustration mounted. He tried to penetrate the depth of his emotions, but always ended up telling himself that his *yetzer hara* also knew how to do the same and could perform a charade of perfection. So how was he ever going to determine whether his feelings were really true?

A few days passed this way, plunged in introspection, until Elimelech finally decided to return to the *Mashgiach* and tell him about his doubts.

Trembling, he entered the room and poured out his heart. He studied the *Mashgiach*'s expression, desperately trying to predict how the *Mashgiach* would react. But the *Mashgiach*'s face remained serious and impenetrable, until Elimelech finished speaking.

Only then, suddenly, did the *Mashgiach*'s face light up with a warm smile. "**This** is what I have been waiting for," he said.

Elimelech looked at him, astonished, and asked, "But is there a way? Will I ever be able to tell the difference between holiness and the schemes of the *yetzer hara*?"

"Yes, indeed," replied the *Mashgiach*. "There's a very direct way: Examine the results."

"What does that mean?" Elimelech asked.

"Tell me, has *Chassidus* impacted your Torah learning?"

"Absolutely!" Elimelech replied. "I study now with much more enthusiasm, and I believe I sense the holiness of the Torah I study."

"No, set aside your feelings," the *Mashgiach* told him. "I'm asking simply whether you learn the same amount and in the same depth as before."

"Yes, even more than before I found *Chassidus*," said Elimelech.

"So there's your proof for its authenticity!" said the *Mashgiach*. "And what about prayer, are you more mindful of the words' meaning as you say them? Do you now concentrate more on your devotion in prayer?"

"Yes, I feel I do," Elimelech confirmed.

"So there you have another proof that, as of now, your desire to study and understand *Chassidus* seems to be true and genuine," the *Mashgiach* assured him.

"Remember this rule well: Anything that leads to a weakening of Torah study, or of *mitzva*-observance, or of devoutness of prayer, even if it comes in a mask of fiery enthusiasm and great excitement, does not derive from holiness. But anything that increases and strengthens all these is surely the proper path. Continue to study *Chassidus*, and may *Hashem* help you."

Full of joy and relief, Elimelech left the room. The *Mashgiach*'s words had introduced him to a new soul aspect that he had never before realized. He started to examine everything more carefully to see whether it was truly authentic and sprang from within. This new approach, he felt, set him upon the "highway" in Torah study and service of *Hashem*.

CHAPTER TEN

L'CHAYIM; L'CHAYIM V'LIVROCHA

Whispered rumors among those attending the *Tanya* class began to be confirmed. The students became more excited as they looked forward happily to the spiritual experience they expected. At the most recent class, Reb Yosef Yitzchak confirmed it officially, announcing that next week, following the lesson, he would hold a Chassidic *farbrengen* to celebrate 20th Cheshvan, the birthday of the Rebbe RaShaB, Rabbi Sholom DovBer (1860-1920), the fifth leader of Chabad and founder of the original renowned *Yeshivas Tom'chei T'mimim* in Lubavitch.

Seeing the glow in all the students' eyes, Elimelech understood that a *farbrengen* must be a remarkable event to which everyone looked forward eagerly. Personally he had already gained some appreciation of a *farbrengen* from the one he had experienced in Haifa at the beginning of his spiritual journey. Although he had some idea what to expect, however, he was looking forward to participating in this *farbrengen* and seeing how Reb Yosef Yitzchak would lead it.

Several aspects of a *farbrengen* still remained problematic for him. Why was the joyous atmosphere so important? Those who led *farbrengens* apparently spoke about serious issues, so surely a serious mood seemed more appropriate. And when concentrating on exalted concepts of serving *Hashem* by refining one's character and devotion to Torah and *mitzvos*, what are a bottle of alcohol and sour pickles doing on the table?

Elimelech found the presence of alcohol utterly baffling. Yes, he was aware of the centuries-long Chassidic custom but figured that drinking *l'chayim* was just a way for Chassidim of old to find encouragement to rise above their difficult day-to-day lives which were so often full of suffering. He understood that, during hard times, Chassidim would attend a *farbrengen*, raise their spirits by drinking *l'chayim* on a little alcohol, while sharing Chassidic teachings to permeate their dark lives with meaning and light. But what place did this have for Torah scholars who studied *Chassidus* daily before praying at length? It all confused Elimelech no end.

When these questions arose in his mind, he recalled that *farbrengen* in Haifa and the uplifted, refined mood prevailing there. It was clearly not just a friendly get-together. Everyone there felt a sense of holy, spiritual inspiration, and sat with such closeness and unity, focusing intently on the words of the *Mashpia*. But why the alcohol? Elimelech struggled with this. Wouldn't the atmosphere be so much more serious and appropriate without such superfluous ingredients?

Elimelech decided to share his questions with Yisroel, who had become his good friend. It was he who explained to him many Chassidic ideas when he felt uncomfortable bothering Reb Yosef Yitzchak. But this time Elimelech was surprised when Yisroel, instead of answering directly as usual, responded instead with a forgiving smile and a parable.

"During the era of the *Beis Hamikdash*, the great Sanctuary in Yerushalayim, there was a Jew in the Holy Land who had never traveled there as the Torah requires, three times a year, for the holidays of *Pesach*, *Shavuos*, and *Sukkos*. He had never been properly educated about the *Beis Hamikdash* and the importance of this *mitzva*, so he never felt the need to go. When neighbors and friends would go up to Yerushalayim, he always had some excuse not to join them.

"But as the years passed, he started to regret his many lost opportunities to fulfill this important *mitzva*. Everyone else went up to Yerushalayim three times a year, yet he had not been there even once. These thoughts bothered him until he finally decided once and for all to see exactly what so inspired everyone to travel to the *Beis Hamikdash* again and again.

"He saddled his donkey and set out. Throughout his long journey, he tried to imagine the *Beis Hamikdash* and what happened there. He decided it must be a place where everyone entered silently with tremendous awe, trembling in prayer before the Creator. The atmosphere must be so spiritual and exalted. It must be place where the entire material world, with all its conceptions, is forgotten and only a spiritual silence prevailed.

"Joyously he reached the gates of Yerushalayim, and with tremendous longing quickened his pace as he approached the *Beis Hamikdash*. As he climbed the Temple Mount, however, the sounds of bleating and mooing gradually filled his ears. He looked around, wondering whether perhaps he had taken a wrong turn. But no, everyone else was walking in the same direction to the top of the mountain.

"When he reached the *Beis Hamikdash* and ascended to its inner plaza, the *Azara*, he was suddenly shocked. Blood covered the full breadth of the *Azara* floor as hundreds of *Kohanim* (priestly descendants of Aharon) ran back and forth, carrying containers of blood. Sheep and cattle were slaughtered, carcasses were being skinned and cut into pieces.

"He was struck speechless, utterly dismayed. Suddenly he cried out, 'This is a *Beis Hamikdosh*? This is a slaughterhouse!'"

Yisroel concluded his parable with a broad smile, without offering further explanation.

Elimelech understood that this parable was intended as a sharp response, and he accepted the rebuke. Later he reflected on the parable's details and sensed even more strongly its vivid message. Indeed, that is how the *Beis Hamikdash* would appear, at first glance, during the time when *korbanos* (offerings) were being brought. To someone with no conception of the great holiness of *korbanos* and what they accomplish on the spiritual plane, how could one describe their sublime importance? Especially is that true concerning a *mitzva* of such seemingly mundane nature, which actually achieves tremendous elevation, as the *Zohar* says, "The mystical secret of *korbanos* ascends up to the mystical secret of the Infinite One Himself!" Someone who does not realize all this can certainly think he has mistakenly arrived in a slaughterhouse.

Perhaps Yisroel was right. It is impossible to describe a *farbrengen*'s special quality. One needs to participate in it and only then can one appreciate this celebration and everything accompanying it, Elimelech concluded.

***

The *Tanya* class proceeded as usual, but one could sense the students' underlying excitement and anticipation for what would soon follow. They did not spend much time asking questions this week, and the class ended at the scheduled hour.

One of the students pulled out a box of refreshments, including a bottle of alcohol and some packages of crackers, which others poured onto a few plates, while some sliced pickles.

Reb Yosef Yitzchak moved forward in his seat. His face looked excited with a shining light. "Say a *niggun*!" he directed. The room filled with a Chassidic melody, somewhat hesitantly at first, but quickly gaining momentum and intensity. Elimelech reflected on Reb Yosef Yitzchak's expression of "saying a *niggun*," rather than "singing." On the surface it sounded strange, but it seemed obvious that, among Chassidim, *niggunim* were **said**, not sung, for a *niggun* had to be sung in a way that it would speak and communicate.

He looked around the room. The students' faces radiated inner joy. Elimelech had always assumed that a *farbrengen* for Chassidim was similar to a *mussar* talk for yeshiva students. Both intended to inspire their audience, foster improvement of personal faults, and encourage positive resolutions for Torah study and serving *Hashem*.

But what a difference there was between the two approaches! The mood of a *mussar* talk was sharp, even threatening, with an undercurrent of sadness. At the *farbrengen*, on the other hand, joy and happiness prevailed. At a *mussar* talk, students would be focused inward, their faces sealed, their eyes frozen. Here, however, the atmosphere was full of vitality, pleasure, enthusiasm and musical rhythm, and everyone's eyes were sparkling. This is a different world entirely, he told himself again and again.

One student assumed the task of pouring alcohol into little cups and distributing it. As each student said *l'chayim*, Reb Yosef Yitzchak locked eyes with him, responding *l'chayim v'livrocha*. He reminded them that the Rebbe had several times forbidden drinking *l'chayim* more than three or four times. "On its own," he stressed, "*mashke* [alchohol] is repulsive. We have no choice, for we need this repulsive substance in order to refine the material body. But it's forbidden to overdo it and there's no benefit in crossing the line, but only a huge loss."

The students continued singing beautiful *niggunim*. There was one of them who seemed be responsible for starting off each *niggun*. Gradually the *niggunim* became slower, more heartfelt and soul stirring. Each *niggun* was sung many times, enabling Elimelech to pick them up and eventually join in and sing along. He began to feel the depth of the *niggunim*. Each melody touched his heart, moving and inspiring him. The atmosphere steadily became more serious and seemingly more demanding, but still full of faith and joy.

Elimelech took a small cup of vodka and said *l'chayim*, which Reb Yosef Yitzchak acknowledged. The sharp liquid burned his throat and he quickly reached for a bite to cancel the bad taste. Now he wondered even more what could be the point of this disturbing custom.

Suddenly, he noticed Reb Yosef Yitzchak watching him. Apparently he had sensed his inner turmoil. At least that was how Elimelech interpreted his sudden explanation of the meaning behind drinking alcohol.

"I don't think I've ever told you the parable great Chassidic masters would give about the importance of saying *l'chayim*," said Reb Yosef Yitzchak. "So I'll share it with you now."

"A great king had an only son who was very dear to him. To give his son the best education, the king entrusted this task to the most outstanding teachers and mentors. The son was a diligent student who studied hard. On reaching adulthood, he had revealed high intelligence, and also excelled in outstanding qualities of character, so that everyone praised him.

"His father, the king, was proud of him. Yet he always wondered whether his son's conduct and manner were really authentically integral to him, or perhaps they resulted from his being present in the royal court. So he decided to test him.

"'At the end of my empire,' the king told his son, 'is a province where the inhabitants are incredibly primitive and coarse, totally unable to grasp the concept of my sovereignty and that they should be subordinated to me. You, my son, are very wise, so I want to send you there to teach the locals to become devoted to me and to influence them to accept my sovereignty.'

"With tears the prince left his father to set out on this lengthy, difficult mission. Arriving there, determined to fulfill his assignment, he was full of confidence as he began speaking with the locals. But all his efforts to describe the great king who lived in a palace, surrounded by the royal court of important ministers, etc., were in vain. The natives were so primitive that they thought he had lost his mind. He became deeply disappointed, for there was no one to talk to.

"The prince realized that to get though to them would require enormous patience. He would need to socialize and sit with them, listening to and participating in their absurd small talk, and only very gradually try to explain in their own terms about the existence of the great king. He started to interact with them and become like them. From time to time he managed to slip in a word about the king and his empire, but then they would always look at him with wide, questioning eyes until he finally despaired of ever accomplishing the mission entrusted to him.

"Over time, he hardly felt how gradually he was becoming more and more influenced by their ways and attitudes. He behaved more coarsely, began to enjoy their inane talk and laugh at their crude jokes, until he became just like them. His life was now as primitive and uncivilized as theirs. He forgot that he was a prince, and his mission faded from his mind.

"Several years passed. One day a stranger suddenly appeared, looking for the king's son. He had brought him a letter sealed with the royal signet ring. The prince froze. In that moment, he recalled that he was someone special, the king's son, entrusted with a special royal mission. Distress filled his heart as he grasped his present sorry situation and how low he had fallen.

"He opened the letter and read his father's encouraging words: 'Surely you are progressing well in your mission. I look forward to the day when my dear son will send me great news about how well you have succeeded in your mission, so that you can return home to the palace.'

"In a torrent of tears, the prince reflected on his miserable situation. He decided that, from now on, he would never let himself forget his goal. His decision and his father's encouraging words in his letter filled his heart with joy. He was so fortunate not be one of those primitive natives; he was the king's son! He felt an intense desire to dance from great joy. But he feared everyone would think he had gone crazy if they saw him dancing on his own in the middle of the day.

"What did he do? He bought a barrel of whisky and invited everyone he knew to a party, where he gave them so much to drink that all became tipsy and jolly and started dancing happily. The prince himself joined them, dancing as joyously as them.

"But there was a deep difference. They were happy with the whisky coursing through their veins, while he was rejoicing in his happiness at being the king's son and being entrusted with a special royal mission. This allowed him to express his great joy by dancing, without anyone thinking he had gone out of his mind!

"This is a very deep parable," Reb Yosef Yitzchak concluded. "It is a parable about the Divine soul within every one of us. It descends from its exalted Heavenly abode into a coarse, physical body. There's a purpose to its descent. Its task is to elevate its animal soul and its physical body, together with the surrounding world, to holiness. But the coarse materiality of the body and the world drown the Divine soul in their lowliness and make it forget its special mission.

"That's why we sit at a *farbrengen*, to recall the Divine soul's true mission in this world. This arouses feelings of remorse and inspiration, but also great joy that 'We are fortunate that our portion is so good,' as we say early in our morning prayers. 'Our portion,' *Chelkeinu*, refers to our Divine soul, which is a *chelek Eloka mimaal mamash* – 'literally part of G-d from Above' (as the Alter Rebbe writes in *Tanya*, Chapter 2). But we also have an animal soul and a physical body that are involved in inane shallowness, and they disturb the Divine soul from revelling in its joy. So, what do we do? We let our body drink some whisky. Then the body and animal soul are happy with the whisky, while our Divine souls can be happy that we are Jews and Chassidim!

"It's important, however, to be careful not to forget the true reason for our joy," Reb Yosef Yitzchak reminded them. "We mustn't let the body's happiness interfere with the happiness of the soul. That's why we must never cross the line. In that way we'll be able to *farbreng* properly and achieve the desired benefit."

The way the *Mashpia* related this parable held the students spellbound. So vividly had he described the prince's mission, what passed through his mind at the various stages of his residence in that primitive province, his distress and then his great joy. As he concluded his account, they all thought deeply on the story's significance.

Elimelech tried to focus on every detail of the parable and its parallels in the analog. The longer he dwelled on it, the clearer the picture became – the experience of the Divine soul, the royal prince, sent into a coarse body in this lowly, material world, struggling to remain attached to its Father in Heaven, *Hashem*.

The *farbrengen*'s atmosphere began, slowly but surely, to penetrate the students' hearts. Their hearts opened to each other, to Reb Yosef Yitzchak's words, to the inner message of each of the *niggunim*. Elimelech felt a change coming over him, not quite sure whether from the vodka or from the *farbrengen*'s atmosphere. He felt a deep closeness with the other students and with Reb Yosef Yitzchak. The words spoken at the *farbrengen* touched him very deeply. He felt a barrier had been lifted from his heart that had previously blocked him from fully accepting everything he heard.

His earlier questions about the character of a Chassidic *farbrengen* now seemed more and more laughable. What would a *farbrengen* be, he thought, without these ingredients? It's the *mashke*, the *niggunim*, the special style that make the *farbrengen* so special. Thanks to all these, a *farbrengen* becomes a setting for true friendship, brotherly love and closeness. It's all these that enable a *farbrengen* to penetrate the heart, to move something deep within. Without them, it would be just a depressing *mussar* sermon.

During a *farbrengen*, Reb Yosef Yitzchak acted very differently than during his class. He spoke with more feeling and warmth, his words more heartfelt and earnest. At this *farbrengen*, there was something new: He started commenting on subjects not generally discussed in public. His audience accepted his words lovingly and in the right spirit, for they were spoken with love. No one became insulted. In that special atmosphere everyone felt united, and no one was embarrassed; no one felt hurt by his mild, loving criticism.

The hours passed quickly. The *niggunim* sung between Reb Yosef Yitzchak's talks seemed to strike ever deeper into their hearts. Each of the students was deep in thought on what had been discussed and how it related to his personal service of *Hashem*. But now they were all waiting. They awaited the rare moments when Reb Yosef Yitzchak would open up and speak about much deeper subjects that he otherwise only hinted at, reserving them for very special occasions.

Indeed, that is what happened in the course of this *farbrengen*.

CHAPTER ELEVEN

REACHING THE TRUTH

The clock had long struck midnight. Outside, a soft wind rustling the leaves on waving branches was the only sound disturbing the stillness of the night. It seemed like an echo to the *Mashpia*'s soft, quiet words, as if the whole creation was sharing its secrets, arousing the soul to serve *Hashem*, reminding every Jew to realize his life's purpose on this earth.

Reb Yosef Yitzchak sat deep in thought, his face flushed. The students were singing a rousingly beautiful melody known as *Niggun Hachona* – "Melody of Preparation" – of which the Rebbe RaShaB was particularly fond. They repeated it over and over again. Such melodies were integral to the *farbrengen*'s special atmosphere, for their exalted message seemed to inspire and demand no less than Reb Yosef Yitzchak's words.

Elimelech gazed at Reb Yosef Yitzchak, and sensed that something was stirring within him. He seemed obviously in another world. His fingers tapping the table lightly to the *niggun*'s rhythm was the only sign he was aware of anything around him.

He had just been explaining at length the immense accomplishments of the Rebbe RaShaB, whose birthday on 20th Cheshvan they were celebrating. He described the Rebbe RaShaB's unique Chassidic discourses, which are distinguished by their amazing breadth and depth, explaining the most exalted concepts of Chassidic philosophy with a striking clarity that anyone can understand. "That's why," he noted, "Chassidim called the Rebbe RaShaB the 'RaMBaM of *Chassidus*.'"

Reb Yosef Yitzchak's focus, however, was on the Rebbe RaShaB's unprecedented innovation in the Chassidic world – indeed in world Jewry – by establishing the renowned *Yeshivas Tom'chei T'mimim*. In addition to the unique character education it gave its students, it was the world's first yeshiva to integrate in-depth *Chassidus* study into its daily schedule, studied the same way and in the same depth as *Nigleh* – Talmud and *Halacha*, etc. Several hours of the yeshiva's daily study schedule, in the morning and the evening, were devoted to *Chassidus*.

When Reb Yosef Yitzchak spoke about *Yeshivas Tom'chei T'mimim*, Elimelech felt he was speaking about something near and dear to him. His face and tone of voice expressed an inexplicable longing, an immeasurable bond. Clearly, *Yeshivas Tom'chei T'mimim* for him was much more than a yeshiva; it was an essential part of his being.

When he fell into a long, meditative silence, it seemed that his sweet memories were flooding through him. He seemed so attached to his yearnings for those precious days he had spent in the yeshiva that the students felt how he had touched some poignant inner chord within his soul. They secretly prayed he would share everything passing through his mind.

***

The melody they sang ceased on its own. Rain had begun to fall, and the drops tapping against the windows seemed to intensify the warmth and enthusiasm filling the room, like a subliminal response to the cold outside. The students became ever more attuned to their inner selves.

Just then, Reb Yosef Yitzchak began to speak. He related about his entry to *Tom'chei T'mimim*, and what was so distinctive about it. He mentioned the renowned elderly *Mashpia*, by now no longer in this world, and other personalities prominent in the world of the *T'mimim*. He described the yeshiva, located in those days deep in a *pardes* (orchard) near Lod, and how it raised pure, complete Jews at a time when so many thought only in terms of defending *Yiddishkeit* against secular onslaught. It was a time when even G-d-fearing Jews felt compelled to compromise to some degree, if only in their dress and outer appearance, in a world so distant then from Torah and *mitzvos*. At the height of that difficult period, he said, *Tom'chei T'mimim* raised Jews totally devoted to *Hashem* with every fiber of their being, Jews who scorned the world and laughed at what it feared, Jews unafraid to approach other Jews on the street or at a *kibbutz* and to say to them: "Be a Jew!"

"What amazed me most when I entered *Tom'chei T'mimim*," he related, "was that, within a short time, I came to realize that the yeshiva demanded my entire self. It demanded that I devote not only hours of study to *Nigleh* and *Chassidus*, not only the time of prayer and *farbrengens*, but also absolutely everything else: eating, sleeping, my free time, my short weeks of vacation, my desires and aspirations, even my small talk – everything!"

When mentioning "small talk," he smiled and told of a friend at the yeshiva who related how he had come to *Tom'chei T'mimim* because of its students' small talk! During his summer vacation one year he had met a few *Tom'chei T'mimim* students and heard their conversations. On comparing what they considered "idle talk" to the conversations he and his friends would have in their spare time, that student had concluded that the "idle words" he heard from *Tom'chei T'mimim* students were reason enough to enroll there.

"The first thing we heard, repeated over and over again," Reb Yosef Yitzchak continued, "was that *Tom'chei T'mimim* demands *p'nimius*, authenticity. For *T'mimim*, the most rejected personality is a *chitzon*, someone superficial, whose inner being does not match his outer expression, who concentrates on his external self while neglecting his inner being. A student who studies enthusiastically during study sessions and prays in a loud voice, but who acts like most people while eating and doing other mundane activities, simply can't exist at *Tom'chei T'mimim*!

"This yeshiva demands a student's entire being, not only that he study well and pray devoutly. It expects him to change his very being, transforming him into a *Tumim*, a Jew complete in all his ways.

"I started to understand the extent of this when the *Mashpia* told about a certain student who applied to enroll in the yeshiva in Lubavitch (later I found the story printed in *Likkutei Dibburim*, which comprises many extraordinary *sichos* of the Rebbe RaYYaTz). This story drilled into my mind awareness of the intense demands directed at the students, the *T'mimim*.

"Whenever a new student applied to study at *Tom'chei T'mimim* in Lubavitch, he had to be accepted by two separate committees. The first gave a face-to-face interview to test his academic skills and level, and to hear him describe his life history and accomplishments to date. This committee then presented a detailed report of its analysis to the yeshiva administration, the Rebbe RaShaB and his son, the later Rebbe RaYYaTz, who served as the yeshiva's spiritual and financial administrator.

"The second committee was covert. It also started working immediately, but a new applicant would have no idea it even existed. No member of this committee ever spoke to him, nor was he ever called to meet with them. Secretly they would track his conduct, how he prayed, how he spent his free time, etc. Then they, too, prepared a report of their impressions about the applicant's inner character. In most cases, apparently, it was the conclusions of the second committee that finalized whether the student was accepted or rejected.

"A young man once applied to the yeshiva. The first committee praised him as a talented scholar, highly recommending his acceptance. But the secret committee noted that his character traits were coarse and his face, too, was unrefined.

"The Rebbe RaShaB expressed special interest in this student because of his fine talents. He perused the two reports several times, giving the matter much thought. Finally, he decided to accept him to the yeshiva but told his son, the RaYYaTz, it would be necessary to 'take him firmly into his hands.'

"It was then in the middle of of the month of Cheshvan. For this student, the RaYYaTz set a particularly severe individualized schedule for the course of the winter, and directed the supervisors overseeing the study sessions to pay this student special attention.

"When *Pesach* approached and preparations began for the matzo baking, in which all the yeshiva's students took part, the

Rebbe RaShaB directed his son to give this student the most difficult responsibilities, but in a way that he would not notice he was being singled out for special treatment.

"For two full weeks, the student had not a moment of rest by day or night. All the most difficult jobs – of inspecting the wheat for possible leavening, preparing the hand-mill, and grinding the grain – were given to him. He asked no questions, for that was a basic tenet in Lubavitch – no one ever asked why or what for. If told to do something, everyone did it without a word.

"When all preparations were complete and the actual baking started, all the most difficult tasks were again assigned to this student. Then, when preparations started for the special matzo baking of the afternoon before *Pesach*, he was again given the bulk of the work. In addition, the Rayyatz gave him the responsibility of checking the yeshiva's office for *chametz*, a job lasting until 2:00-3:00 in the morning. By 7:00 a.m., he had to be present for his turn at the matza bakery.

"On the afternoon before *Pesach*, at 5:00 in the afternoon, not long before the holiday's start, the Rayyatz summoned the student and directed him to study the discourse starting 'Sheishes Yamim' (published in the Mitteler Rebbe's collection of his father's discourses on the *Siddur*), telling him that he would study the discourse with him the next morning at 7:00. He was well aware that the student had been appointed as leader of one of the students' tables at the *Pesach seder*, and that until the *seder*, which would not end before 2:00 in the morning, he would not have even a quarter-hour to study. This was a most difficult trial, to test how precious *Chassidus* study was for this student.

"When the student entered the RaYYaTz's room next morning at 7:00 a.m., the discourse was well absorbed in his mind, relative to his level of knowledge of *Chassidus* at the time. The RaYYaTz studied with him for an hour. Then he went in to speak to his father, the Rebbe RaShaB, to give him a full report. The Rebbe was pleased. 'With *Hashem*'s help,' he said, 'we have planted a tree that will bear fruit. I hope he will absorb the right attitudes to the extent that he will come to influence others, too. It may take much more time, but in the end his tree will have many branches, bearing plentiful fruit, which will, in turn, produce further produce.'

"On the last day of *Pesach*, the *Seudas Moshiach* – the feast in honor of *Moshiach* – was held in the yeshiva's study hall, with the Rebbe's participation. The Rebbe delivered a discourse of *Chassidus*, after which the participants danced joyously until late at night. At that festive meal, the Rebbe RaShaB looked at that student and said to his son, 'Yosef Yitzchok! Look at the effect of perspiration for the sake of a *mitzva*. He face has been utterly transformed. The coarseness has gone and his face now looks like that of a *mentsch*.'"

"Indeed, that student became a great Torah scholar, *Rav* and *Rosh Yeshiva*, renowned for his wisdom and also his Chassidic refinement."

The students at the Reb Yosef Yitzchak's *farbrengen* were riveted by this inspiring story.

"Such is the education that builds a *Tumim*," he continued. "Torah study is only one aspect of that education. *Tom'chei T'mimim* was not founded to establish just another yeshiva for studying Torah. There were plenty of those, and it was not for that purpose that such great effort was expended in establishing this yeshiva. It was founded in order to raise a G-d-fearing generation of Jews permeated with love and awe of *Hashem*, for whom the inner Torah and inward service of *Hashem* would define their entire being, a generation who would save the Jewish nation throughout the heavy darkness of the final days of exile before *Moshiach*'s coming. For such a goal, it's not enough just to study Torah. It requires a fundamental inner education that permeates the student's inner core.

"Whoever examines what our Rebbes have said and written about *Yeshivas Tom'chei T'mimim* understands immediately that it's far more than a yeshiva in the usual sense. One can quote dozens, even hundreds, of instances when they expressed a unique vision for the purpose and important role of this yeshiva.

"In a well-known talk, the Rebbe RaShaB used the following words: 'I have been guaranteed – everyone knows the difference between being certain and being guaranteed – that the students of *Tom'chei T'mimim*, wherever they will be, will actualize, with utter self-sacrifice, the Divine intention of *Hashem*'s desire to have for Himself a dwelling in the lowest world.'

"In that same talk, the Rebbe RaShaB made a unique covenant with the yeshiva's current and future students: 'The students of *Yeshivas Tom'chei T'mimim*, who presently study in all its departments, and who will study in it in the future, those who are here and those not yet here – I am making now a covenant with you, a covenant of participation in serving *Hashem* with utter self-sacrifice for the Torah and awe of G-d, and service of

Hashem with the heart, without concessions or compromise, to the ultimate extreme...'"

This was the first time Reb Yosef Yitzchak has ever spoken openly to his *Tanya* class about *Tom'chei T'mimim*. In the past, he had deliberately avoided speaking about it, so that the class should not seem to be a recruiting station for *Tom'chei T'mimim*. Repeatedly he would emphasize that, in the present generation, study of *Chassidus* is obligatory for every Jew and has nothing to do with the type of yeshiva where one studies.

In some cases he had even expressed opposition to certain students transferring to *Tom'chei T'mimim*, saying they were not ready for it and did not appreciate what such a step would mean. He told them to continue studying at their present yeshivos, while continuing to study *Chassidus* at his classes. If eventually they would still feel that, without transferring to *Tom'chei T'mimim*, it would hinder their growth in Torah and service of *Hashem*, perhaps then it could be discussed.

In the light of his usual silence about the yeshiva, his lengthy discussion now came as a total surprise to the students. His words, apparently, had just poured out of his heart without him even intending to speak so openly. He seemed to be reliving anew his years at the yeshiva, and his words had flowed out in a stream of deep emotion. He described at length the *farbrengens* led by the *Mashpi'im*, the yeshiva's special approach to *Nigleh* study, the heartfelt prayer of the students known as *ovdim*, who prayed devoutly, often for hours, with the result that their entire being was permeated with unique seriousness.

But one central theme ran through all his words: "From the moment we entered the yeshiva," Reb Yosef Yitzchak declared, "everything began to revolve around a single theme – how to arrive at the truth. How could our words of prayer truly express the feelings of the heart? How do we ensure that our enthusiasm for studying the Torah is a true passion stemming from the Torah's holiness? How do we become men of truth in all our thoughts, words and actions?

"That's when the real work began. Until then, we had always been pleased with ourselves. *Boruch Hashem*, we studied the Torah, fulfilled *mitzvos* beyond their basic requirement, prayed with devotion, treated our friends kindly. Our general goal was always to grow, to advance further, continuing on the path we had lived until then.

"But then came *Yeshivas Tom'chei T'mimim* and slapped us on our faces. As soon as everything was compelled to pass through the burning test of truth, it became clear that we remained woefully short of our potential. Now we realized where we stood and how far we were from the truth! When we watched the aged *Mashpia* sitting with us at a *farbrengen* and crying bitter tears as he expressed his deepest wish to finally arrive at the truth, we began to understand what he meant and how truly far we were from the truth.

"Our aspirations utterly changed. Our previous sense of smug self-satisfaction dissipated, and we began to view everything in its right dimension. All our previous false illusions and distorted assessment of what was important now seemed laughable and ridiculous. We suddenly understood what kind of toil we would need in order to achieve anything, in order eventually to be privileged to fulfill the Divine purpose for which we were created in this world."

The *farbrengen* concluded as the first rays of dawn started to shine through the windows. At loss for words, the students left and went on their way, each silent and introspective. Elimelech's heart burned with a strong desire to come closer to the fascinating spiritual world spread before him at the *farbrengen*.

It was too late to go to bed. Instead, Elimelech entered his yeshiva's study hall and studied *Tanya* enthusiastically for several hours, oblivious to everything around him. Reviewing the chapters he had learned in the class, he tried to instill the subjects deep into his heart. That morning, after the inspiring *farbrengen* and his *Tanya* study, his prayers were different than any prayers he had ever experienced. Reaching the blessings before the *Sh'ma*, he felt for a moment that his inner inhibitions had broken open, as something different and very warm, deep and true, burst forth.

CHAPTER TWELVE
WHAT DID *CHASSIDUS* INNOVATE?

The study week in yeshivos runs from Sunday to Thursday, all day and through the evening. On Friday, studies usually end around noon, leaving the afternoon off to prepare for *Shabbos*.

That Friday, Elimelech used his free time to visit a Torah bookstore. For some time, he had been upset by all the time often wasted waiting for basic Torah books that students consulted regularly, particularly those frequently quoted by the yeshiva lecturers in their lessons. There was always a long line to use these books, such as commentaries on the Talmudic tractate studied that year, and students often waited long for a turn to consult them. Elimelech decided to free himself of the endless frustration, and had been saving his pocket money to buy his own copies of the volumes most used.

Going through his list at the bookstore, he soon had a nice pile of the books he sought. Finding he still had some money left over, he looked for some other interesting Torah book to buy, and soon ended up in front of the section for *Chassidus* and *mussar* works that he so loved.

As he browsed through the shelves, he heard someone calling him excitedly.

"Elimelech! Is that you? *Boruch Mechayeh hameisim*! 'Blessed is He who brings the dead to life'! Where on earth have you disappeared to?"

He spun around to see his old friend Aharon coming up behind him.

"It's so good to see you!" he exclaimed. "How are you doing?"

"You're asking how I'm doing?" Aharon asked, still excited. "It's been three months since you disappeared into thin air. I didn't even know where to look for you!"

"Well, *boruch Hashem* that He has finally led us to meet again," Elimelech smiled. He quickly chose one of the books he was interested in and, together with the rest of his pile, brought them to the counter and paid for them.

They left the store and found a nearby *shul* where they could exchange notes about their past few months' experiences. Their yeshivos were studying the same Talmudic tractate that year and, with youthful excitement, they repeated to each other Torah insights heard from their Talmud lecturers and *Roshei Yeshiva*. Each was interested in the other's approach to understanding the *Gemara*, and for a long while both enjoyed discussing their Torah studies. Only the fact that *Shabbos* was not long off forced them finally to finish their conversation. They agreed to meet again that evening, after their *Shabbos* meals.

Aharon had much on his mind to discuss with Elimelech. It was Elimelech who had opened the door to his own inner world, and their long conversations had forced him to confront many concepts more penetratingly, to delve into the underlying fundamentals of the Torah and *mitzvos*, and to arrive at a more profound and all-encompassing worldview of *Yiddishkeit*. Elimelech's disappearance had halted this process at its very height. Since they had parted, Aharon sometimes felt like a bird just learning to fly, when suddenly its wings are clipped.

His conversations with Elimelech had been so thought-provoking. Every discussion had led him to think and reflect, to delve deeper. When Elimelech left, he felt this process had stopped. No one was there to arouse him to relate to and examine everything as it demanded. For him, Elimelech had served as a sort of lantern, suddenly lighting up issues in his immediate world to which he had never given a second thought.

Until he had become close to Elimelech, he had not really been aware of the existence of various approaches within *Yiddishkeit* that deal with its most profound concepts and try to set a path before a Jew to establish an inner connection with *Hashem*. Of course, he knew there were various paths, but that awareness was very general. He had never felt it constituted any challenge for him, requiring his close attention.

His world had been been narrowly focused on yeshiva life. His attention had concentrated exclusively on study of *Gemara* and its commentaries. His general purpose was straightforward – to become a Torah scholar and live as a Jew, to study, pray and fulfill the *mitzvos*.

Suddenly, his conversations with Elimelech had opened his eyes. He began to discern the great complexity of everything, the subtlety and fine differences between concepts. Everything that had once seemed so simple and clear, now suddenly became infinitely involved. This glimpse into what lay behind Torah study, into the depth of prayer, into the roots of the *mitzvos*, aroused a storm within him. All of a sudden, he felt the need for a mentor who could clarify and illuminate for him the proper path.

In the past, Aharon had felt, and now even more strongly after his reunion with Elimelech, that the latter had long ago passed the stage where he himself was now groping in relative darkness. Elimelech seemed already to have clarified for himself some basic fundamentals and found his path to follow in life. To some degree, Aharon regarded Elimelech as a teacher-companion. Yes, while he was a companion, he yet hoped to learn from him, to reach the point Elimelech had already passed.

**

Unusually for him, Aharon hurried through his *Shabbos* meal and left right after *Birkas Hamazon*. His inner thoughts gave him no rest. All his disturbing questions and doubts of the last few months returned and gripped him in a maze of confusion. One after the other, he recalled everything he had pondered on so painfully as a result of Elimelech's unfortunate absence from his side, depriving him of the chance to share it all with him.

Walking through the quiet streets calmed him somewhat. There was something magical in the late-night stroll, with the clear sky strewn with stars, like a canopy for the *Shabbos* Queen. From houses along the streets wafted sounds of *zemiros*, the traditional *Shabbos* hymns. The rare passers-by, dressed in *Shabbos* finery, walked slowly along the street, completing the sense of holiness. Aharon made his way through it all silently, deep in thought.

He was relieved to be the first to arrive at their agreed meeting place. Just as before his original conversation with Elimelech, he felt again an excited anticipation, although, as then, he was unsure where to begin. He felt an overwhelming need to discuss, but had no idea how to open the conversation.

When Elimelech arrived, however, he alleviated Aharon's problem. Getting straight to the point, he told him in detail about everything at his new yeshiva, and also about the *Tanya* class he regularly attended, especially about the great impression Chabad *Chassidus* was having on him.

Aharon was thunderstruck. "If I understand you correctly, you're about to become a *Chassid*!" he exclaimed incredulously.

"That's certainly possible," Elimelech confirmed.

"But that's not our traditional path!" Aharon declared emphatically. "We were born to parents of Litvish, non-Chassidic ancestry, we've studied at Litvish yeshivos, and we've been educated in the Litvish path. It's our obligation to continue on that path, and we shouldn't be seeking new paths for serving *Hashem*."

"This isn't a new path," Elimelech answered calmly. "It's the path of the Baal Shem Tov and his holy disciples."

"I'm not negating the validity of the Chassidic approach," Aharon clarified. "It's a good, holy path for those whose ancestors have followed it. But we have a different path. Yes, we may well adopt beautiful aspects of the Chassidic approach, but our basic path has to remain the Litvish path, as the verse [in *Mishlei*-Proverbs 1:8] emphasizes, 'Do not abandon your mother's teachings.'"

"If your premise were correct," Elimelech replied, "the entire Chassidic movement could never have come into existence at all!"

"How's that?" Aharon asked.

"Because all those who became disciples of the Baal Shem Tov and followed his path were not born Chassidim," Elimelech explained. "When someone became a follower of the Baal Shem Tov, he had to make fundamental changes from the path in which he was raised and educated."

"Well, perhaps they weren't acting properly by doing that," Aharon argued. "How do you know they were actually doing the right thing?"

Elimelech smiled. "What you consider to be their possible 'mistake' gave the world *Chassidus* Chabad and Rabbi Levi Yitzchok of Berditchev, the *Noam Elimelech* and Reb Zusia of Annipoli, the Kotzker acuity and the *Sefas Emes*, among so many other greats. If not for their 'fateful mistake,' *Yiddishkeit* would not have been graced with these great leaders, scholars and saints."

"I'm not going to judge previous generations," Aharon conceded. "But I'm still not going to change my mind. In our generation, each has the obligation to follow the path on which he was brought up and educated. If everyone would start searching on his own for some other path to follow, who knows where we would all end up!"

"I'm not sure your assumption has any basis in reality," Elimelech replied pensively. "We're not dealing here with some new-fangled way of life invented by just anyone for himself, but approaches to life well-trodden and well-paved by some of the greatest Torah leaders of all time.

"But let's set that aside for now. What do you say to the claim of *Chassidus* that it's a gift to the entire Jewish people and that every Jew is now obligated to study it?"

"If you're asking what I say to that," Aharon replied, in a serious tone, "I would answer in full honesty that it's presumptuous for *Chassidus* to think it's saved the world. Chassidim seem to think that, without *Chassidus*, Torah and *mitzvos* would no longer exist. I'm simply unable to accept that. I'm not minimizing its importance; I'm well aware *Chassidus* has saved thousands of Jews and kept their *Yiddishkeit* alive. Nevertheless, just like *Chassidus*, there are many other paths within *Yiddishkeit* and many other great Torah leaders who were not Chassidim, yet they too saved and revitalized *Yiddishkeit* for many Jews."

"You know, actually I do understand this claim of Chassidim very well," Elimelech retorted. "I agree absolutely with the statement that *Chassidus* brought an entirely new light into the Jewish world. Your comparison to other approaches within *Yiddishkeit* makes no sense. There's no way to compare the Jewish world before the light of *Chassidus* illuminated our people to after its appearance. Following the revelation of *Chassidus*, everything utterly changed."

Aharon did not answer. He thought about the chasm starting to open between them. Suddenly, he and Elimelech had become two opposing sides in a heated debate.

Elimelech, too, was silent. Similar thoughts must be passing through his mind, Aharon thought. He realized now how far his world was from Elimelech's. But the shock he had felt on hearing that Elimelech was growing so close to the path of *Chassidus* was gradually easing. Instead, he started to experience curiosity and a desire to understand this surprising phenomenon.

So often, Aharon reflected, students at the yeshiva mentioned *Chassidus* and Chabad, yet no one knew how to define its perspective clearly. Whatever they said was based on assumptions or hearsay, on scraps of rumor without basis. Perhaps this is my chance to get to the bottom of it, to understand exactly the approach of *Chassidus* in general and of Chabad in particular.

From his end, Elimelech felt uncomfortable. The course of the conversation, which seemed to have turned him into the fervent *Chassid* justifying *Chassidus*, made him laugh at himself. He was not yet ripe enough for that role, he felt. His inner thoughts and deliberations were not yet fully ready for a situation where he had to communicate the concepts articulately to others. He also knew that Aharon would not be easily convinced, and the challenge scared him somewhat. He decided not to try and convince his friend. On the other hand, against any question implying an attack on *Chassidus*, he felt compelled to respond.

Following the brief silence, however, Elimelech was pleased with Aharon's next question. Their discussion's amiable tone returned, the aggressive argumentation calmed down, and it was back to a pleasurable conversation. Elimelech realized this discussion might even be to his benefit, forcing him to clarify concepts for himself much better. Now he could welcome the challenge.

"Let's try to understand an expression regarding *Chassidus* that I've often heard," Aharon started, "like '*Chassidus* innovated' and '*Chassidus* infused new light.' What exactly did *Chassidus* innovate?"

"You want to know what *Chassidus* has innovated?" Elimelech laughed. "Well, I'll ask you: What hasn't it innovated? What remained the same after *Chassidus* was revealed?"

"I don't understand what you mean," said Aharon. "What did it innovate about the *mitzva* of *esrog*, for example? Do Chassidim use lemons instead of *esrogim* on the holiday of *Sukkos*?"

"You didn't get what I said," chuckled Elimelech.

"Okay, but seriously," Aharon repeated. "On what basis do Chassidim claim that '*Chassidus* introduced a new light'? Are Chassidim really so different from those who are not Chassidim! *Boruch Hashem*, we all study Torah, we all fulfill *mitzvos* carefully and try to pray devoutly. According to what you're saying, it sounds like someone who isn't a *Chassid* has left *Yiddishkeit*!"

"You've brought up a fascinating point," Elimelech smiled. "It reminds me of what happened from time to time in my family when we were kids. My mother would come home with shopping bags full of goodies. She'd put everything down in the kitchen and go to her room for a few moments. Meanwhile, we children would pounce on the bags and empty them all. When she'd come out of her room, we'd ask her innocently, 'Mommy, what did you bring home with you?'

"*Chassidus* accomplished a far-reaching rejuvenation in Jewish life, completely transforming it into a new world. Over time, each of the various traditional groups among the Jewish people came and adopted some of its ideas and practices as its own. And now they come and ask, 'What has *Chassidus* innovated?'"

"That's a very bold, sweeping statement," said Aharon. "Give an example of what you mean."

"Examples!" Elimelech responded. "Sure! Take song and joy. Today you won't find a single yeshiva where they don't sing joyously on *Shabbos* and other special days. Tell me, do you know any melodies from the time before the appearance of *Chassidus* or any sung by those who opposed the Baal Shem Tov. You yourself are laughing at just hearing the question.

"In stark contrast, Jews until today sing countless songs attributed to the Baal Shem Tov and his holy disciples. From this you see clearly that song and joy were distant from the Jewish world in the period before *Chassidus*, and that this is a Chassidic innovation. In our time, everyone has adopted this idea. You can even see the connection between *Chassidus* and song and joy in the fact that traditional Jewish songs today are all called Chassidic songs..."

"Okay, but that's really an interesting example of a relatively minor point," Aharon said. "It's far away from innovations in every aspect of Jewish life."

"I don't think the concept of joy is minor," Elimelech insisted. "Torah and *mitzvos* accompanied by joy are utterly different from Torah and *mitzvos* enveloped in melancholy. But, if you really think it's minor, I'll give another example:

"If the *maggidim* – itinerant preachers – at the time of the Baal Shem Tov would come to life today and enter any yeshiva, even the most Litvish of them all, during the *mussar* study session, they'd certainly be convinced they had landed in a yeshiva of Chassidim. Do you have any idea what those *maggidim* preached in those days? Their sermons were full of fire and brimstone, predicting dire punishments for everyone's sins, and arousing fear and terror in their audiences. All their sermons revolved around that negative theme.

"It was *Chassidus* that introduced a new approach, inspiring listeners with themes of the exalted essence of every Jew, the preciousness and beauty of Torah and *mitzvos*. Their speeches were replete with sayings of our Sages and meaningful explanations that uplifted and gladdened the heart and enriched their listeners' mind, inspiring them to serve *Hashem* with renewed devotion.

"Now, tell me, which approach is most accepted today by the successors of those who originally opposed the Baal Shem Tov and his disciples? Do they continue the approach of the *maggidim*, full of fire and brimstone, or have they adopted the opposite approach, of warmth and light, like that of *Chassidus*?"

"I must concede that you seem right on that point," Aharon agreed.

"Now I'll say something that may really shock you," Elimelech continued. "Until now I've described the general non-Chassidic approach to inspirational speeches and sermons. But do you know where *Mashgichim* and *baalei mussar* in Litvish yeshivos today take the content of their *mussar* talks, their most powerful points, richest explanations, and deepest concepts, the source of most of their ideas? You may not want to believe this, but it's largely from *Chassidus*. Yes, they draw from the works of the Maharal of Prague, too, and other great works of Jewish thought. But *Tanya* and the Lubavitcher Rebbe's *sichos* are among their major sources!"

"Can you bring proof to verify that revolutionary assertion," Aharon demanded.

"You're right," Elimelech accepted his point. "I need to prove what I said. But it's difficult to do that because you haven't yet studied any *Chassidus*. If you study it a little, you'll immediately realize that the same wonderful ideas your *Mashgichim* repeat time and again actually come from explanations found in *Chassidus*.

"I'll give you one outstanding example. The well-known *mussar* work, *Michtov MeiEliyohu*, is regarded as non-Chassidic. But it's full of countless Chassidic concepts, mostly from *Tanya*, as often indicated in the footnotes. The author was an earnest *baal mussar*, open to the truth wherever he could find it. For many years he was active in the Jewish community of England, where he became close to distinguished Lubavitcher *Rabbonim* and Chassidim who introduced him to *Tanya* and Chabad *Chassidus*, which deeply fascinated him. Some have noted that many more passages in his works are based on *Tanya* and other Chabad sources, but some of his editors, apparently aiming to minimize the extent of his Chabad influence, omitted many of these sources.

"So you see that the content of many *mussar* works and *shmuessen* and their concepts, on which we base our lives and Torah attitudes, are actually drawn from *Chassidus*. Once we realize this, it's a bit ridiculous to ask what *Chassidus* has innovated. After so many non-Chassidic Torah leaders have adopted the best of what *Chassidus* has to offer, you ask what it has innovated!"

"Are you actually saying that the power of the ideas and fundamental Chassidic concepts you've mentioned – and many others as you've implied – that non-Chassidim have taken from *Chassidus*, is what keeps the entire *Yiddishkeit* going," Aharon tried to summarize Elimelech's words, "and that this is the contribution of *Chassidus* to the entire Jewish world?"

"To a great extent, yes," Elimelech confirmed.

"I really need to think about all this," Aharon said, a storm of emotions raging within him.

CHAPTER THIRTEEN
THE GREAT CHALLENGE

The more Aharon thought about what Elimelech had told him, the more infuriated he became. The last person he had expected to hear all this from was Elimelech. When he had complained that *Chassidus* presumes to persuade every Jew to study its teachings, thereby restraining them from continuing in the path of their ancestors to whom the path of *Chassidus* was alien, he had been sure Elimelech would take it back and apologize. It never occurred to him that instead he would hear a passionate defense of this Chassidic position, and with such intensity.

True, when Elimelech had explained himself, his explanation had not sounded so threatening. The implied sharpness was softened by reason and logic. Once Aharon returned to his yeshiva, however, his anger mounted. So that's what the Chassidim really claim, he thought, incensed, that, without *Chassidus*, *Yiddishkeit* couldn't endure and it's otherwise impossible to live as a Jew today. That's what they think, that all the holy yeshivos and our era's tremendous expansion of Torah learning and religious Jewish commitment is an outcome of the revelation of *Chassidus*. On what basis do they have the audacity to make that claim?

It pained him to hear all this specifically from his erstwhile friend Elimelech. He had not known him to be shallow or inclined to repeat empty slogans and sensational headlines. On the contrary, he had always considered Elimelech to be well-balanced, intelligent and sensitive, never saying anything before examining it intellectually from every angle. This time, though, it seemed Elimelech had not considered his words carefully enough before saying them. There was no other explanation, he thought, for otherwise how could he possibly have said all that?

They had arranged to meet again on the following *Shabbos* evening. All that week, Aharon could not stop thinking about the subject. Elimelech's explanations had not convinced him, but it bothered him much more that Elimelech even held such opinions. His deepest desire now was to make Elimelech realize how wrong he was, and how dangerous was the implication of his words.

***

At his end, Elimelech sat in the following Thursday's *Tanya* class struggling to focus. Last week's conversation with Aharon would not leave his mind. He felt deeply how difficult the challenge had become. At first he considered washing his hands of the whole affair, telling Aharon he no longer wished to debate him on such sensitive topics. But immediately he rejected that thought. Aharon was no ordinary yeshiva student pestering him with questions. In the recent past they had been close friends, seriously examining together various spiritual problems, searching for answers, seeking the true path to serve *Hashem*. How could he reject him now?

What he had told Aharon during their last conversation now worried him. He was aware how his words may well have upset Aharon, who might not yet have been ready to hear them. Perhaps what he had said should have come only after some preparation. It was clear Aharon had not accepted his words, and Elimelech now wondered whether he should have said what would not be properly received.

He decided to discuss the whole matter with Reb Yosef Yitzchak. Anxiously, he waited for the *Tanya* class to end, and hoped the other students would not ask too many questions that evening. But he was disappointed. They would not give up their usual after-class discussion, which was often more interesting than the class itself. Reb Yosef Yitzchak would use the opportunity to tell various stories and details about Chassidic history, which the students swallowed eagerly.

It was close to midnight when Reb Yosef Yitzchak finally left for home. Elimelech, his heart beating furiously, approached to ask whether he could walk him home while they discussed something on the way. Reb Yosef Yitzchak agreed and slowed his pace as they walked together.

Elimelech told him briefly about his friend Aharon and their spiritual journey together until they had parted ways. He told about last week's chance meeting in the bookstore and full details of their *Shabbos* evening discussion, trying not to leave anything out, for he wanted the *Mashpia* to get a full picture of everything. Reb Yosef Yitzchak listened attentively.

After Elimelech finished, Reb Yosef Yitzchak remained quiet, deep in thought. As they continued walking, Elimelech breathed in the cool night air, which seemed to energize him. He waited patiently for his teacher to respond.

"Your friend must be furious right now," Reb Yosef Yitzchak began to speak softly. "Undoubtedly, you have shaken up his world, openly challenging many of what had been his most basic assumptions. During your conversation, he probably didn't absorb the full implications of what you said. Now you can expect a sharp response from him. Based on your description, your friend doesn't seem the type to let what you said pass without reacting.

"Nevertheless," Reb Yosef Yitzchak continued, choosing every word slowly and carefully, "in my opinion you acted properly. You spoke the truth, and that is most important. The worst thing is to stammer out some murky words that are unclear and apologetic. What we believe with all our heart, and which we are obligated to share with others, we need to say in its entirety, without whitewashing or hiding anything, but pleasantly and peacefully.

"It's important to remember that we aren't speaking our own ideas. We didn't invent this approach, nor was it we who decided to publicize it. These are directives of all the Chassidic leaders, from the Baal Shem Tov and his disciples up to our own Rebbes, the leaders of *Chassidus* Chabad. All have emphasized that *Chassidus* is not a faction or a path for just one group or another; it's a way of life revealed by *Hashem* for the entire Jewish people. It's the revelation of a new illumination, like none before it, which *Hashem* has given to shine for every Jew. The very coming of *Moshiach* depends on *Chassidus*, as he told the Baal Shem Tov – related in the Baal Shem Tov's famous published letter – that he would come 'when the wellsprings of your teachings will spread outwards.'

"This truth needs to be repeated to every Jew, without adornment. There is no reason to apologize for it or to evade the issue. It's the mission the leaders of *Chassidus* have entrusted to us, and we, who study their teachings and follow in their path, have the duty to fulfill their desire and try to pass on this message to every Jew, from the lowest to the greatest."

"That's fully acceptable," said Elimelech. "But I also emphasized that the continued existence of *Yiddishkeit* is dependent on *Chassidus*, and that, thanks to the teachings of *Chassidus* that have spread widely among the entire Jewish nation, *Yiddishkeit* continues to exist. I do understand how irritating that idea is to one who doesn't consider himself connected to *Chassidus*."

"I don't see why that should be considered so terrible," Reb Yosef Yitzchak responded. "Many non-Chassidic Jewish leaders, in the past and present generations, have expressed the exact same point, and much more clearly and sharply than you did. Whoever refuses to accept that fact is either ignorant of recent Jewish history or deliberately blind!"

"But people ask," Elimelech continued, "how can one say that, without *Chassidus*, the Torah would have been forgotten by our nation? Aren't Torah and *mitzvos* strong enough to withstand historical upheavals?"

"Let's ask a simple question," Reb Yosef Yitzchak answered. "During the period of the *Tannaim*, the Sages mentioned in the *Mishna*, suppose one Jewish community would have refused to study the *Mishna*, claiming these were new ideas, and would have just continued studying the Written Torah, the Scriptures and their oral explanations, as had been the norm until Rabbi Yehuda *Hanassi* composed the *Mishna*. Would the Torah have endured in that community?"

"Of course not," Elimelech agreed, "because if it had been possible for the Torah to endure without the *Mishna*, he wouldn't have written it."

"Exactly!" Reb Yosef Yitzchak continued. "And later, if a faction among the Jewish people had refused to accept the *Gemara*, continuing to study the Written Torah and the *Mishna* without the *Gemara*, would the Torah have endured among them?

"So, on the lines of your question," Reb Yosef Yitzchak concluded, "isn't the Written Torah strong enough, or isn't there enough power in the *Mishna* to withstand everything? But this is the order that *Hashem* has arranged for the gradual revelation of the Torah, first the Written Torah, then the *Mishna*, then the *Gemara*, and so on. Why, then, only when it comes to *Chassidus*, do all these questions and doubts arise? Is it impossible to understand that this is the next step in the natural sequence of the Torah's revelation, the stage when its inner dimension, *P'nimius HaTorah*, is revealed?"

"Why, indeed?" Elimelech wondered.

"I don't know," Reb Yosef Yitzchak replied candidly. "The only answer must be that now we're in the era of *ikvesse diM'shicha*, 'the footsteps of *Moshiach*,' when the darkness is so pervasive that all kinds of accusations arise in the Heavenly Court against the revelation of that part of the Torah that has the power to overcome the darkness of the exile. That's the sole explanation that can possibly explain the strangely fierce opposition towards *Chassidus* in the past, and the fact that awful fabrications and false libels have been believed by good and upright people. After all, nowadays it's universally agreed that the original opponents to *Chassidus* were mistaken. It's the darkness of the exile. I have no other way to explain it."

"What would have been if that opposition had never have happened," Elimelech wondered, "and *Chassidus* had been able to spread unhindered to reach every Jew? Would the Jewish people now be in a different situation?"

"How can you even ask that question?" Reb Yosef Yitzchak exclaimed. "First of all, if that had happened, then the whole Jewish people would long have been living in the Holy Land with *Moshiach*, and serving *Hashem* in the third *Beis Hamikdosh*. But even if *Moshiach* had been delayed for some reason, G-d forbid, and we'd still be in exile, there's no doubt that the painful spread of secularism and of so many Jews being far from the Torah and *mitzvos* would be very limited or non-existent. The Chassidic leaders have made very clear that *Chassidus* is the healing balm for all spiritual maladies in these generations. Certainly, if the Jews would imbibe the 'medication,' the disease would vanish!"

They reached Reb Yosef Yitzchak's home. Elimelech was eager to take advantage of the moment to continue talking freely and openly with his teacher. He decided to ask one more question that bothered him.

"But some argue that *Chassidus* innovated concepts that never existed before, which is why all the opposition exists."

"That's most surprising," Reb Yosef Yitzchak smiled. "*Chassidus* didn't innovate anything at all. It only infused life into the Torah and *mitzvos*, and reawakened many ideas that had been ignored or become dormant. It's ironic that the same *Chassidus* which revived many original Jewish concepts is condemned as innovative by those same Jews whose customs are themselves innovative and whose approaches and perspectives have veered somewhat from the original, mainstream *Yiddishkeit*. I'm referring to things like melancholy and depression, remaining aloof from some other Jews, etc. Now they come and blame *Chassidus*, which returned the original joy of *Yiddishkeit* and its original love of fellow Jews, with inventing something new!"

"How can we prove that?" Elimelech asked.

"Come inside," Reb Yosef Yitzchak invited him in. "Let me show you some interesting things."

They climbed the stairs to Reb Yosef Yitzchak's apartment. Elimelech felt uncomfortable when his teacher prepared him a cup of tea and set some cookies before him. But Reb Yosef Yitzchak did it without a second thought and immediately continued their conversation.

"I'll show you proof of what I said, based on three ideas that many consider to be innovations of *Chassidus*. One is joy. The second is that everyone should serve *Hashem* in every facet of life, not only when studying or praying but even when involved in business or while eating and drinking. The third is the Chassidic approach to true service of *Hashem*, that one need not break or afflict his body but, on the contrary, when the body is healthy and strong, and one's lifestyle in no way harms the body's needs, that's when his service is complete. These are three areas viewed by many as innovations of *Chassidus*.

"Now I'll show you whether that's really true," Reb Yosef Yitzchak said. From his huge bookcase, he removed three volumes.

"We first mentioned joy. You may know that the greatest of the Kabbalists, the *Arizal*, Rabbi Yitzchok Luria (1536-1572), who lived several centuries before *Chassidus* appeared, has a well-known explanation of the verse (*Devarim* 28:47), 'Because you did not serve *Hashem*, your G-d, with joy and a glad heart.' The verse is not stressing that 'you did not serve *Hashem*.' On the contrary, you did serve Him, even with all your might, but not with 'joy and a glad heart.' And that's the reason for the severe punishment of 'you shall serve your enemies.'

"Okay, that's the *Arizal*, a Kabbalist, but we're seeking proof from *Nigleh*, the revealed Torah of the Talmud and Halachic authorities. So here's the *Rambam*, one of the greatest Halachic authorities of all time, accepted by everyone; see what he gives as a Halachic ruling in the last paragraph of *Hilchos Lulav*:

"The joy with which a person should rejoice in fulfillment of the *mitzvah*, and in love of *Hashem* who commanded them, is a great [spiritual] labor. Whoever holds back from this rejoicing is worthy of retribution, as is stated: '...because you did not serve *Hashem*, your G-d, with joy and a glad heart.' Whoever holds himself proud, giving himself honor and acting haughtily in such situations, is a sinner and fool. Concerning this, King Shlomo warned [*Mishlei*-Proverbs, 28:10]: 'Do not seek glory before the King.' [In contrast] anyone who lowers himself and makes his body agile in these situations is the [truly] great person, worthy of honor, who serves G-d out of love. Thus, David, King of Yisroel, declared [Shmuel II, 6:22]: 'I will hold myself even more lightly esteemed than this and be humble in my estimation,' because there is no greatness or honor other than rejoicing before

G-d, as stated [ibid., 6:16]: 'King David was dancing wildly and prancing before G-d.'"

"So you see, *Chassidus* can't claim to have innovated in this area," Reb Yosef Yitzchak said. "The *Rambam* wrote this many centuries earlier.

"Now let's see who introduced the approach that it's possible and necessary to serve *Hashem* in everything we do."

Reb Yosef Yitzchak opened the *Rambam*'s *Sh'moneh Perakim* ("Eight Chapters" – his introduction to his commentary on *Pirkei Avos*), to Chapter 5:

"One's only intention in eating, drinking...sleeping, awaking, moving about and resting should be the preservation of one's bodily health. The purpose of bodily health is that the soul should have healthy and perfect limbs in order to acquire wisdom, and attain moral virtues and intellectual qualities until it reaches that ultimate goal... Similarly, when involved in gaining money, one's ultimate goal in its acquisition should be to use it for exalted pursuits and to spend it on his bodily needs so that he will continue to live, until he will grasp and know about G-d what is possible to know... Meaning to say that he should use all faculties of his soul, and direct them only towards the purpose of knowing G-d, and he should do no act, small or great, nor speak any word, unless that act brings to a higher purpose, or to what can bring to a higher purpose... This is what G-d demands of us to have in mind when He states (*Devarim* 6:5), 'You shall love *Hashem,* your G-d, with all your heart, and with all your soul, and with all your might,'meaning to say, with all your soul's faculties, that you should make every faculty of it to have a single purpose, the love of G-d. The Prophet has already exhorted this same point [*Mishlei*-Proverbs 3:6]: 'In all your ways know Him.'"

"So, did the Baal Shem Tov introduce this idea?" asked Reb Yosef Yitzchak. "Is this an invention of *Chassidus*? Here you see that the Baal Shem Tov invented nothing; he just repeated the words of the great *Rambam*.

"Now I'll show you something that, if you wouldn't know its source, you'd be absolutely sure it's taken straight from some work of *Chassidus*. The Baal Shem Tov's explanation of the verse [*Shmos* 23:5], 'When you see your enemy's donkey,' is well-known: When a person pays attention to the *chomer* [physical material] of his body [similar to the Hebrew word for donkey — *chamor*], he may think it's his enemy [for it desires everything that's the opposite of spiritual]. So he might assume 'he should refrain from helping him,' and instead break it with fasting and self-mortification. But the Torah instructs us instead, 'You shall surely help him' — by protecting it and assisting it to be healthy and whole. Do not break the body, but refine it. That's what the Baal Shem Tov teaches. Now look at the identical content in — believe it or not — the TaZ, the *Turei Zohov*, one of the main commentaries on the *Shulchan Oruch*, a century before the Baal Shem Tov."

Reb Yosef Yitzchak opened a *Shulchan Oruch, Even Ho'ezer*, at the beginning of Chapter 25, and showed Elimelech the words of the *TaZ* there:

"We find that the *Rambam* writes on the verse, 'In all your ways know Him,' that it means that whoever eats and drinks, and gives his soul pleasure in order to be healthy and strong to be able to serve *Hashem*, he has the same reward as one who fasts. This concept is based on another verse [*Tehilim-Psalms*, 127:2]: 'It is futile for you who rise early, etc.' There are Torah scholars who limit their sleep to study much Torah, and there are Torah scholars who sleep a lot so they will have the strength and alacrity to study Torah. In truth, such a person can study in one hour what that other one who caused himself suffering can accomplish in two hours. Surely their reward is identical. Concerning this the verse states, 'It is futile for you,' implying that it is purposeless for you to cause yourself suffering by rising early and sitting up late at night to minimize your sleep; it is purposeless, because 'He provides as much for His loved ones while they sleep' [ibid.]. To one who sleeps a lot to strengthen his mind in Torah, *Hashem* gives his portion in Torah identical to the one who sleeps very little and causes himself to suffer, etc."

Elimelech smiled, "That's amazing. It sounds like a real Chassidic insight!"

"These are just three isolated examples, and there are many more like them," Reb Yosef Yitzchak observed. "There's a clear, explicit source in *Nigleh* for every concept in *Chassidus*. There are no innovations. This is the answer to whoever asks what you just asked me earlier. *Chassidus* invented nothing. It only brought to life parts of *Yiddishkeit* that were dormant, and added inner meaning and depth. The real question is not why did these concepts become aroused in *Chassidus*, but how did they become dormant before the rise of *Chassidus*?"

***

Elimelech returned to yeshiva elated. Now he was ready for tomorrow evening's conversation with Aharon. His teacher had provided him with strong fundamental concepts, which he now proceeded to review and develop in his mind during the hours remaining until their meeting.

CHAPTER FOURTEEN
THE SOUL AND SPIRIT OF LIFE

Aharon got straight to the point. After a polite "Good *Shabbos*," Aharon told Elimelech, "I still consider you a good friend. That's why I'm going to speak to you very openly."

"What are you referring to?" asked Elimelech, thrown off guard. He had not expected their conversation to start like this.

"Wait," said Aharon, a serious expression on his face. "Don't interrupt me till I've finished everything I have to say. I've given hours of thought to what you said last week. I'm emphasizing this before I start so you won't think I'm reacting impulsively to what I heard you say. Believe me, there are very few things to which I've given such serious thought as I have about this subject.

"I hope you won't be insulted when I tell you that, in my opinion, you're being drawn further and further towards the most extreme views of some Chassidim, and you don't fully realize the implications of what you're repeating. The words leave your mouth easily, and you don't seem to grasp how extreme they are. Try to recall where you were standing just a year or two ago, and look at what you said from that vantage point; maybe then you'll see the other side of the argument.

"Basically you implied that you completely negate the entire existence of the Litvish approach, including all the great scholars who have established and nurtured it. According to you, only the Chassidic approach has the right to exist among the Jewish people; everything of value derives from it and draws from it, every Jew gets his Jewishness from it and all are obligated to adopt its ways and accept it entirely! How can you possibly say that?

"Look how far you've been drawn towards such an extreme, narrow view. Instead of seeing each branch of the Jewish people as a component of a single structure, which enriches all of us with its multi-colored array, you've categorized everyone into two groups of black and white, one of which is those who are positive, with all the rest being mistaken, G-d forbid. As a good friend, I advise you to re-examine anew what you've been hearing in your *Tanya* classes, and to try to view everything from a broader and truer perspective."

Aharon finished speaking and took a deep breath. He carefully watched Elimelech's face, anxiously awaiting his response.

Elimelech started to realize how he had shocked his friend last week. Now he felt distinctly the wide chasm separating their two worlds in such stark opposition.

He didn't answer right away. A heavy silence hung between them. His brain searched feverishly for the right approach to convince his friend of the truth of his words. He had a fleeting thought that perhaps he should just avoid this whole sensitive topic altogether, but immediately remembered Reb Yosef Yitzchak's unequivocal insistence, that despite the difficulty, he had the duty to share these ideas without whitewashing or evading the issues.

So he decided to focus his answer on one central point. He argued forcefully that the time had come finally to put an end to the last traces of the unfortunate opposition that had arisen against *Chassidus*. Even the *Rambam* had to deal with incredible opposition, he reminded, but eventually it had subsided. Ultimately not a single Jew remained who did not regard the *Rambam* as the "great eagle," by whose words we live. Yet regarding the revelation of *Chassidus*, although everyone acknowledges that the reasons for the original opposition were mistaken, and everyone agrees it has infused powerful inspiration among all levels of our people, nevertheless there remain vestiges of opposition and those who still say they have no connection to *Chassidus*.

"This attitude should be eliminated, because it's simply wrong," he concluded. "*Chassidus* is a gift that *Hashem* revealed for every Jew, to enable us to stand strong against the intense darkness of the era of *ikvesse diM'shicha*, "the footsteps of *Moshiach*," and to taste the great light of the *Geula*. *Chassidus* is not meant for a specific group or community, but it belongs to the whole Jewish people. That's why I keep repeating the same message that there's no Jew who can exempt himself from studying the teachings of *Chassidus*."

Elimelech's words helped Aharon realize he had been too harsh in his judgment. While Elimelech was firm in his position, he clearly realized the implications of his words. Although this still annoyed Aharon somewhat, nevertheless it persuaded him to make the effort to understand Elimelech's position concerning *Chassidus*.

"Let's say I would accept what you're saying," he said with a smile. "What would you expect me to do? Is it your goal that I leave my yeshiva and go enroll in a Chassidic yeshiva?"

"Not at all!" Elimelech replied. "That idea never occurred to me. If you're asking me what you should do so that the light of *Chassidus* can shine in you, the answer is simple: Go study it. Study *Chassidus*!"

"And how would you answer the argument that one first needs to gain a solid foundation of Talmud study and *Poskim* – the codes of Halachic law – before learning *Kabbala*?" Aharon asked.

"I would answer first that *Chassidus* is not *Kabbala*, about which there are rulings for the appropriate age and stage in life to be able to study it," Elimelech said. "But I don't want to get into that now. The main point is that *Nigleh*, the revealed Torah, which you called 'Talmud and *Poskim*,' is compared by our Sages to bread, while *P'nimius HaTorah*, the Torah's inner dimension, is compared to salt. We find this in the *Gemara* (*Shabbos* 31a): 'This is comparable to a man who says to his representative, "Bring a measure of wheat upstairs." He went and brought it up. He said to him, "Did you mix salt into it for me?" He said to him, "No." He told him, "It would have been better if you had not brought it up."' Bread without salt can't last. Therefore, specifically because of the importance of study of Talmud and *Poskim*, everyone should study *Chassidus*, so that their study of *Nigleh* will be in the right spirit."

"So what happened during the generations before *Chassidus* appeared?" Aharon questioned.

"Those generations had loftier, more sensitive souls," Elimelech answered. "They found the 'salt' in *Nigleh* itself, in the non-Halachic passages of *aggada* – the inspirational material included in the Talmud, with much additional similar material in the various works of *Midrash*, etc., all of which are also considered *P'nimius HaTorah*. That's why they didn't need specifically *Kabbala* and the material included in *Chassidus* – which was the very reason why *Chassidus* was not publicized in those generations, because there was no need for it. But in these later generations, when we are on a much lower spiritual level – a point on which everyone, Chassidim and non-Chassidim alike, agrees – there's no way to study Torah properly, with authentic awe and love of *Hashem*, other than by study of *Chassidus*."

"That's what you say!" Aharon exclaimed indignantly.

"No, this isn't my invention," Elimelech shot back heatedly. "It's what all the great Chassidic leaders have said. Indeed, Rabbi Chaim Vital, the *Arizal*'s main disciple who wrote down all his teachings, writes the same, in very sharp words, about the absolute obligation to study *P'nimius HaTorah*. The Vilna Gaon writes the same, in his commentary on *Mishlei* [20:9] and in other places in his works. The *Arizal* expresses it in these words: 'In these later generations, it is permitted and imperative to reveal this wisdom.' So what I said is very well-founded!"

"Nevertheless," Aharon argued, "the heads of the Litvish yeshivos have never accepted this in practice, and have not taught *Chassidus* in their yeshivos."

"Do you really expect me to answer that question?" Elimelech asked. "Do you want me to tell you it's just another example of the same miserable vestiges of resistance to *Chassidus*?"

Aharon kept quiet. Despite all his attempts to poke holes in Elimelech's approach, he realized how strong and tight was his logic. Elimelech was presenting a world that stood in total opposition to his own, yet this world was complete from every direction. For his every question, Elimelech had a clear, logical response. Ironically, this only intensified Aharon's desire to recognize his friend's views more thoroughly.

"Let's assume you're correct," he started again, going back to their original conversation. "But I still don't see how *Chassidus* has made any sort of innovation. For every point you make, you find sources from the *Gemara*, *Halacha*, and great Torah leaders who lived before *Chassidus*. So, what did *Chassidus* innovate? What's this 'new light' of *Chassidus*?"

"You've cut straight to the central point of it all," Elimelech smiled. "It's actually a question Chassidim have dealt with for many generations. Our *Mashpia* told us that Chassidim were once sitting at a *farbrengen* and asked the same question: 'What did *Chassidus* innovate?' One of the Chassidim sitting there answered, '*Chassidus* innovated the *bracha*, 'shehakol nih'yah bid'varo!' The other Chassidim turned to him in astonishment, 'That blessing was instituted by our Sages thousands of years ago!' He responded, 'The innovation of *Chassidus* is that the words of that *bracha* are really true – that everything exists by His word!'"

"To prove to you I'm not so ignorant of Chassidic stories," said Aharon, with a mischievous sparkle in his eye, "I once heard a similar story about one of the great Chassidic leaders who, as a young man, traveled to study under the Mezeritcher Maggid, the leader of the Chassidic movement after the Baal Shem Tov. After remaining there for some time, he returned to his father-in-law, a *misnaged*, opponent of *Chassidus*, who was sure his son-in-law was straying from the Torah path. But he was surprised to see that his son-in-law was as careful with *mitzva* observance as before and studied Torah as intensely as before.

"Curious, he asked him, 'I see you're acting just as you did before you went to Mezeritch, so what did you gain by going there?'

"His son-in-law answered, 'Now I know there's a Creator of the world.'

"His father-in-law was shocked, 'Only now you know that?'

"He called in the house maid and asked her, 'Tell me, is there a Creator of the world?'

"'Of course,' the maid answered, 'there's a Creator of the world.'

"He asked his son-in-law, 'For this you had to travel to Mezeritch, to find out something that even our maid knows?'

"His son-in-law answered, "She says it. But I know it! That's why I had to travel to Mezeritch."'

"That's a great story," Elimelech laughed. "I least expected to hear it from you."

"I've already told you I have nothing against *Chassidus*," Aharon told him. "I'm open to hearing beautiful things anyone has to share, but I can't accept the attitude that everyone has to study *Chassidus* and that without it it's impossible to be a G-d-fearing Jew."

Elimelech did not answer. It was pointless to repeat the same explanations again and again. An oppressive silence hung over them. But Aharon quickly reopened the conversation. "Let's go back to a topic we once spoke about: You claim that *Chassidus* innovated a concept of Jewish thought, explaining secrets of creation and *Hashem*?"

"Yes and no," Elimelech answered. "No, because Jewish thought on our beliefs has always existed, long before *Chassidus* appeared. That literature is known as *Chakira*, Jewish philosophy. But yes, because *Chassidus* transformed that study into something entirely different."

"So tell me what did it actually innovate?" asked Aharon impatiently. "You keep on skirting the issue and avoiding giving me an answer. Tell me clearly: Did *Chassidus* innovate something, and if so, what was it?"

"It's a very deep subject," Elimelech said, starting to get serious. "To properly explain it, I need first to tell a story I heard on this subject. Rabbi Shneur Zalman, the author of *Tanya*, once sat with his grandson, who later became the renowned *Tzemach Tzedek*, on his lap.

"Rabbi Shneur Zalman asked his grandchild, 'Where's Grandfather?'

"The child pointed to his grandfather's hand and said, 'Here's Grandfather!'

"The *Baal HaTanya* said, 'That's Grandfather's hand, but where's Grandfather?'

"The child pointed to his head and said, 'Here's Grandfather.'

"But the *Baal HaTanya* said, 'That's Grandfather's head, but where's Grandfather?'

"The grandson pointed to various parts of his grandfather's

body, and his grandfather kept on repeating that these were individual limbs, but where was Grandfather?

"Suddenly, the child jumped off his grandfather's lap and ran to hide behind the door.

"'Grandfather, Grandfather,' he called.

"'Yes, what is it?' his grandfather asked.

"But the little boy repeated, 'Grandfather, Grandfather,' until finally, the *Baal HaTanya* got up from his seat and walked over to him.

"When his grandson saw him, he exclaimed, 'Here's Grandfather!' He thereby expressed that his grandfather's entire existence, as he was alive and complete, was the definition of who he was."

"Are you trying to say," Aharon asked, "that the innovation of *Chassidus* is expressed in the fact that it constructed a comprehensive system out of all the disparate fundamental concepts that already existed before?"

"That's true," Elimelech concurred, "but it's more than that. Let's examine this profound story more deeply. When you ask what a human being is, you can answer that he's a creature who stands upright. You could also say he's a creature with the ability to speak. You could argue that he's a creature with a mind that can grasp abstract, refined concepts. You could list all special qualities unique to human beings. But the true answer is that he includes all these qualities when he's alive and functioning. A corpse also has all his limbs, but he's no longer a person. A person is defined by the life expressed in all his limbs and qualities.

"Now, let's revisit the whole idea of *Chassidus* and the stories we've just told, in which the greatness of *Chassidus* is emphasized by how it clarifies profound concepts – that's the head of *Chassidus*. The inspiration and joy *Chassidus* brings – that's the heart of *Chassidus*. The special care in fulfilling *mitzvos* that results from commitment to *Chassidus* – is the 'hands and feet' of *Chassidus*. On their own, however, none of these is the definition of *Chassidus*. *Chassidus* is the vitality, the soul, of all these different aspects. When anything is infused with a soul, it's transformed into something entirely new and different, alive and vibrant.

"Delving into the secrets of creation existed long before *Chassidus*. The obligation of love for every other Jew is a fundamental concept that has existed since the Torah was given, long before *Chassidus*. The innovation of *Chassidus* is that it blew a spirit of life into all these and turned them into something alive and animated."

"You're using words that are undefinable. What do you mean, 'it blew a spirit of life'?"

"And what's the soul?" Elimelech retorted. "Can you define what keeps anyone alive? The soul is not definable, but that's no proof it doesn't exist. The Torah, too, has a 'body' and a 'soul.' The *Zohar* says that its body is *Nigleh* and its soul is *P'nimius HaTorah*, which *Chassidus* reveals. When you study *Chassidus*, you're permeating yourself with the spirit of life of *P'nimius HaTorah*."

"To sum it up, you're unable to define what *Chassidus* is," smiled Aharon.

"No one can define the essence of *Chassidus*, because it's beyond definition," Elimelech replied. "But we see its effect and the energy with which it infuses us. *Chassidus* is like the soul of Jewish life. It's the spirit of life of the Torah and its *mitzvos*."

"And someone who doesn't study *Chassidus* isn't alive?" Aharon asked sharply.

"I'll tell you another story, and then you'll understand my answer," replied Elimelech.

"The *Gemara* and *Halacha* specifies that, during the 'Ten Days of *Teshuva*' from *Rosh Hashana* until *Yom Kippur*, we should be very careful to pronounce the letter *lamed* of *l'chayim* in the words *Zachreinu l'chayim* ('Remember us for life') specifically with a *sh'va* vowel, not a *patach* (which would be *lachayim*) because the latter could be misheard as *lo chayim*, 'not alive,' and during those 'Awesome Days' when our destiny is being weighed in the Heavenly Court, we need to be extra careful about what comes out of our mouths.

"Based on this, when we recite the prayers of *Geshem* (on *Shmini Atzeres*) and *Tal* (on the first day of *Pesach*), when saying the words *L'chayim v'lo lamovess* ('For life and not for death'), why do we pronounce the letter *lamed* of *lamovess* with a *patach* vowel, which could be misheard as *lo movess* – not death?

"Once, at a *farbrengen*, a prominent *Chassid* gave his own answer to this question: 'We pray to *Hashem* to be privileged to live a life full of vitality, not just a life that is 'not death.' He explained that some live a life that is only 'not death.' But we want to be truly alive. To ensure that we don't get to that point, we need to study *Chassidus*, because without it, we might well live a life that, although it includes Torah and *mitzvos*, is merely 'not death.'"

"I see that the gap between my perspective and yours is too wide to bridge," Aharon sighed. "Still, I'm interested in finding out more about the approach of *Chassidus*."

Elimelech shrugged. "You and I both have much more to learn before we truly understand *Chassidus*. These concepts are very deep."

Aharon gazed at his friend and sensed a wall rising up between them. It pained him. With all his heart, he wanted to stay away from debates and triumphalism. But he felt that both he and Elimelech were firmly entrenched in their views and refused to meet the other halfway. His mind searched for a way to renew their old companionship, and with these thoughts he parted from Elimelech.

CHAPTER FIFTEEN
PHILOSOPHIZING

During the past year or two, Aharon's close friends had been Bentzion and Elimelech. His friendship with Elimelech had come to an abrupt halt when he disappeared, going to study at a different *yeshiva gedola*. Although their recent reunion had been an opportunity to renew their friendship, Aharon was now realizing how far apart they had become. In their conversations and debates, their common language had seemingly collapsed as the differences in their worldviews became more sharply pronounced with each interaction.

The only one with whom Aharon had been able to share his thoughts after every emotionally charged debate with Elimelech was Bentzion, to whom he would repeat the discussions they had, sharing his frustrations and disappointments. Together they would analyze Elimelech's outlook and propose responses to his arguments.

Lately, however, Aharon had a sense that Bentzion, too, was drifting, and felt he might be losing him. His close companion and study partner had been showing increasing interest in works of Jewish thought and philosophy. At night and during lunch breaks he would seclude himself in the yeshiva library looking through books such as the *Kuzari, Moreh Nevuchim* and works of the *Maharal*. He would also peruse various periodicals and leaflets lying around that gave answers to questions about Jewish faith and thought.

This new pursuit wrought deep change in Bentzion. He began to engage classmates in all kinds of debate on various philosophical questions, continuing these conversations for hours without tiring. Even his Torah study and entire thought process acquired a philosophical bent. At first he tried drawing Aharon into it all, but his study companion showed no desire to get involved in philosophic subjects; he considered it a foolish phase which would pass as quickly as it had appeared.

To his chagrin, however, it did not seem to be passing so fast. His companion's questions were not a passing phase but were actually deep-rooted, stemming not from curiosity but from inner torment. They gave him no rest. He could spend hours and days seeking an answer to a specific question and, once he found it, his mind was already seeking answers to his next question.

The more this saga dragged on, Aharon started becoming very concerned. He had often heard about the spiritual dangers of this path. True, he himself was occasionally bothered by various such questions, but he always forced them from his mind, determined to reinforce his simple faith. But he felt now that Bentzion's philosophical investigations might cause him harm.

Every passing day seemed to confirm his fears. He sensed a certain coldness creeping into his Bentzion's heart. It was as if his natural spiritual sensitivity had become dulled, and his characteristic innocence seemed to have evaporated. More and more, Bentzion was viewing everything from a purely intellectual perspective; gone was the deep soul bond with which he used to study Torah, pray and recite *Birkas Hamazon*, or fulfill any *mitzva*.

Repeatedly, Aharon pleaded with Bentzion to abandon his philosophical research. But it was in vain. Bentzion always responded that was impossible for him to leave his questions unanswered; he just had to resolve his doubts.

"Who says you need to understand everything?" Aharon tried convincing him. "We are small people, incapable of getting to the bottom of such concepts. On the contrary, most likely we will err and distort what we assume we understand, and what we lose will far outweigh what we gain. It's much better to believe with simple faith in everything written in the Torah and in the words of our Sages, and absolutely to ignore such questions and doubts."

"You may be right," Bentzion responded, "but I just can't ignore and distract my mind from what really bothers me. If I don't try to find the explanations and answers to the questions that trouble me, they'll surely continue to fester and no benefit will come from that. I have no choice. I must clarify these issues for myself."

"But you see how your involvement in it makes you apathetic and affects your *yiras Shamayim*, your religious sensitivity," Aharon would rebuke sharply. "What will be the end of this process? Don't you realize the danger you're getting into? Leave philosophy alone and focus on learning Torah. All your questions and doubts come from the *yetzer hara*. The *Gemara* says *Hashem* tells us, 'I have created the *yetzer hara*, and I have created for it the Torah as its antidote.' Take advantage of every moment to study Torah, and you won't have time to think about all these questions of faith!"

Bentzion gave no reply to this argument, for he knew his friend's words to be true. Aharon was right that, since Bentzion had started researching these subjects, he had fallen spiritually. Sometimes he gave in to Aharon's pressure and renewed his devotion to his studies enthusiastically. But after just a few days, he would find himself distracted, his thoughts returning to those same spiritual subjects.

Once, when Aharon returned from his conversation with Elimelech and told Bentzion all about it, an idea occurred to Bentzion. He still sought to find some justification for his philosophical research, and now a great opportunity appeared to find it.

"Tell me," he asked Aharon, "what impression do you get of Elimelech's spiritual condition in Torah study and *yiras Shamayim*? Does he learn Torah as enthusiastically as he always did, and is he as religiously sensitive as he was when he was together with us in the *yeshiva ketana*?"

"I haven't noticed that he has become any lower spiritually," Aharon said. "We spoke a lot about our Torah studies, and it seems to me that he's learning very intensively. No, no negative changes have happened to him. On the contrary, his faith and *yiras Shamayim* seem stronger."

"And that's even though he's learning *Chassidus*," said Bentzion, with an ironic smile.

"So what?" Aharon responded with surprise. "Did you ever hear me say that *Chassidus* might lead one away from following *Yiddishkeit* properly? I clearly consider *Chassidus* to be a fine, holy path. What I do emphasize to him is that, just as *Chassidus* is a holy path, so are there other paths in *Yiddishkeit* no less holy and true."

"Okay," Bentzion continued, his smile widening, "but what does he study in *Chassidus*?"

"I don't understand what you're driving at," Aharon parried, try to guess at Bentzion's drift. "What question is that – what's he studying? He's studying *Chassidus*!"

"Fine!" Bentzion would not let up. "But what is that? What does he study in those classes?"

"Look, you've already heard his answer to that," Aharon laughed derisively. "He claims that *Chassidus* is the 'soul.' He studies about 'vitality,' 'soul', things like that... Obviously he couldn't explain to me what is that 'vitality' he's talking about..."

"Set that aside for now." Bentzion became serious again. "He's studying **something**, trying to understand certain concepts. Which subjects is he examining, in your opinion?"

"It's probably esoteric ideas, about the *maaseh merkova* [Divine chariot] or *maaseh breishis* [creation], which the *Rambam* refers to," Aharon replied mockingly. "But believe me, these subjects, as fascinating and enchanting as they may be, don't particularly interest me. All I know is that 'the secret matters belong to *Hashem*,' as the Torah says. We have only the Torah that has been revealed to us: the *Gemara*, *Rishonim*, and *Acharonim*. All the rest is none of my business."

"Okay," Bentzion explained, "but here's a student studying philosophical subjects and delving into profound questions, yet you yourself admitted you haven't seen any negative effect on him!"

Suddenly Aharon grasped where Bentzion was leading him. "*Chassidus* has no similarity to the philosophy you're pursuing," he blurted out, almost unthinkingly.

"Why do you say that?" Bentzion asked. "Why aren't they similar? How do you know there's any real difference between them?"

"You're right. I don't know," Aharon admitted, somewhat perplexed. "*Chassidus* is a complete, structured approach to serving *Hashem*. It must have rules and fundamental approaches for how to study it. You can't compare such a complete, well-trodden path to your personal investigations in philosophy."

"You're wrong," Bentzion argued stubbornly. "Am I inventing my own ideas? What am I studying, after all? I am reading the works of great Torah authorities. This, too, is a well-trodden path. Can't I rely on the *Rambam* and Rabbi Yehuda Halevi?"

"I don't know what to tell you," Aharon said, not to be swayed from his position. "I have never been involved in these subjects. But I do believe it's dangerous for you to study them. You can't be sure you understand the subjects properly."

"Elimelech, too, can never be sure he understands correctly," Bentzion defended himself hotly. "For that matter, even you can't be absolutely sure you understand the *Gemara* page properly."

"Enough, leave me alone!" Aharon raised his voice and concluded the argument. "Address your questions to people greater and wiser than I. In my opinion, everything you've said is just a self-justification for this wild whim that's overtaken you!"

Bentzion understood exactly what his friend was telling him. He knew that, in many ways, Aharon was right. Whenever he tried to answer Aharon's arguments, he realized he was just grasping at any possible way to explain himself. The anger with which Aharon ended their conversation forced him to recognize that matters had come to a head. The option of making excuses was over.

It was now clear that it was imperative for him to re-examine his study of philosophy objectively without avoiding the outcome. If he could find sufficient validation for his study, then he would be able to continue. If not, he was obligated to cease immediately, without any evasion.

Yet it was difficult to make the decision alone. He felt a need to consult with someone greater than himself whom he could respect. A few times he almost plucked up enough courage to approach the *Rosh Yeshiva* or *Mashgiach*, but always got cold feet at the last moment. It was obvious to him that they would unequivocally forbid him to study philosophy. He wanted to consult with someone who could see the positive in his philosophical search.

The idea that suddenly struck him like lightning seemed crazy at first. He himself was shocked when the thought occurred to him. But the more he considered it, the more reasonable and realistic it became. Finally, he made his mind up to go with it: He would discuss his problem with... Elimelech's *Mashpia*!

Aharon was utterly shocked at the idea, unable to digest it. When he recovered, he wondered whether his friend was serious or perhaps it was one of his jokes. How characteristic of Bentzion to come up with such bizarre schemes!

"Is he the only person you can think of to consult?" he asked scornfully.

"You know, it'll certainly make for an unusual conversation," said Bentzion enthusiastically. "It'll be interesting to hear what someone like him has to say about my question."

"What will he tell you?" Aharon rolled his eyes. "He'll tell you to leave philosophy alone and to study *Chassidus* instead."

"That would be excellent!" Bentzion rubbed his hands together. "If he says philosophy is dangerous and the solution is *Chassidus*, I'll demand to hear the difference between them: Why is studying *Chassidus* permitted, while philosophy is forbidden."

Aharon was much less excited by Bentzion's plan, but the challenge secretly pleased him, too. He told Elimelech of Bentzion's wish to speak with his *Mashpia*, and a few days later, Elimelech gave his teacher's affirmative response.

***

Right after the yeshiva's evening study session, Aharon and Bentzion walked out and started their walk to Reb Yosef Yitzchak's home. Until now, Aharon had been unsure whether to join Bentzion in his conversation with Elimelech's *Mashpia*. He really wanted just to stay in yeshiva and study, dismissing Bentzion's problems from his mind. But his concern for his friend's spiritual welfare made him feel the importance of being at his side during this possibly fateful stage, and he decided he could not let him go alone.

As the two walked quickly together, Bentzion voiced his thoughts aloud: "What's the best way to start the conversation with Reb Yosef Yitzchak?" With Aharon's agreement, he chose an indirect method of communication as the best plan of action.

Elimelech awaited them at the door, and brought them inside, where Reb Yosef Yitzchak welcomed them warmly.

Reb Yosef Yitzchak's natural warmth and obvious wisdom made a favorable first impression on the two friends. Within moments, the feeling between them was pleasant and relaxed. After they exchanged polite pleasantries, Reb Yosef Yitzchak fell silent, waiting for Bentzion to speak.

Bentzion started hesitatingly. "In recent months, I've been very bothered by questions of faith and spirituality. These doubts pester me without relief and it's painful; they trouble me no end and disturb my life as a yeshiva student. I thought that perhaps you could help me find answers to my questions."

Reb Yosef Yitzchak did not reply at first. Deep in thought, he studied Bentzion's face. Reb Yosef Yitzchak's penetrating gaze made Bentzion feel somewhat uncomfortable and gave their meeting a most serious feeling.

"And you?" Reb Yosef Yitzchak turned suddenly to Aharon. "Are you, too, bothered by doubts and questions of faith?"

"Not at all," Aharon hurried to respond, feeling some sense of alarm. "These things never, ever bother me. I believe in everything with simple faith."

"So then why are you bothered by these matters?" Reb Yosef Yitzchak turned back to Bentzion. "Why don't you believe with simple faith, without a need to philosophize and ask questions?"

"We seem to have different personalities," Bentzion sought a good explanation to an unexpected question. "Aharon, apparently, is able to ignore such questions and to distract his mind from them. I just can't. I've tried but failed."

"Would you describe yourself as an analytical person?" Reb Yosef Yitzchak softened his tone.

"I think so," Bentzion agreed.

Reb Yosef Yitzchak thought for a while, his expression still solemn. Finally he turned to Bentzion. "It would be worthwhile for you to study *Chassidus*. It will strengthen your belief."

"Will I find answers to my questions in *Chassidus*?" Bentzion asked, with a meaningful wink towards Aharon. The conversation was proceeding exactly as he had anticipated.

"*Chassidus* will strengthen the faith in your heart," Reb Yosef Yitzchak replied. "And if there will still be a need for various answers, you'll be able to find them in *Chassidus*."

"What do you mean to say?" Bentzion tried to understand. "I'm searching for answers and explanations for questions that bother me. Will I find them in *Chassidus*?"

"Yes, but that's not the main point," Reb Yosef Yitzchak reiterated. "The main point is that you need to strengthen your faith, and *Chassidus* will strengthen the faith in your heart."

"How, by giving me good answers?" Bentzion felt he was not quite grasping the point.

"Not necessarily," Reb Yosef Yitzchak replied. "You can find answers in works of Jewish philosophy."

"If so, wouldn't it be worthwhile to study those philosophical works?" asked Bentzion.

"Definitely not," replied Reb Yosef Yitzchak sharply. "The Rebbe RaShaB, the fifth leader of Chabad-Lubavitch, once on *Simchas Torah* evening gave a yeshiva student who studied philosophy a slap on his cheek, commanding him to stop those studies immediately."

"Why? What's so bad about philosophy?" Bentzion asked.

"It's a fact that philosophy has left many casualties in its trail," Reb Yosef Yitzchak replied. "Many who got involved in it over the centuries became heretics, and for many others it cooled off their faith. The reality has proved that, in so many cases, it causes a descent in *yiras Shamayim* and in one's ardor for holiness, which is why some of the greatest Torah authorities prohibited study of philosophy, particularly for young people."

"I don't understand that," protested Bentzion, who had not expected such strong opposition from Reb Yosef Yitzchak against study of philosophy. "Surely Jewish philosophy explains so much and answers so many questions. Why would it weaken anyone's faith? On the contrary, it would seem to strengthen one's faith!"

"Perhaps philosophy can benefit someone who already suffers from issues with his faith," Reb Yosef Yitzchak explained.

"His faith has already been weakened, and for him the danger incurred by studying philosophy may be worthwhile on the chance that philosophy might help him. This is obvious from the title the RaMBaM gave his philosophical work, *Moreh Nevuchim*, 'Guide for the Perplexed,' because it was intended for those already perplexed. But for someone not in such a state, it's absolutely **not** advisable to have any contact with philosophy."

"But why?" Bentzion pleaded.

"Because philosophy causes intellect, to some degree, to take the place of faith," Reb Yosef Yitzchak explained. "Whatever one had previously accepted naturally by faith has now become transformed by philosophy into a cold, intellectual concept. Intellect does not have the warmth and power that faith possesses. Faith is the Divine soul's limitless recognition, which is why faith is also unlimited. But intellect is always limited. Even the most logical explanation is never stronger than the degree of logic within it. A more compelling reasoning can always take its place. That's why natural, limitless faith is incomparable to limited intellectual conclusions."

Aharon and Bentzion listened attentively to Reb Yosef Yitzchak with growing fascination. They never imagined that he in particular would so vehemently oppose deep intellectual pursuit of answers to spiritual questions and would insist on simple faith. The obvious question was on the tip of their tongue, but Reb Yosef Yitzchak forestalled them.

"Now you're going to ask me, so why do we study *Chassidus*?" Reb Yosef Yitzchak smiled. "Doesn't *Chassidus*, too, explain things intellectually and bring lofty concepts of faith down to the level of understanding and knowledge?"

Aharon and Bentzion nodded.

"The answer is a bit subtle," Reb Yosef Yitzchak started to explain. "First, let's look at the facts on the ground. Simple reality proves the extreme difference between *Chassidus* and philosophy.

"The Rebbe RaShaB had a brother, Reb Zalman Aharon, known by Chassidim as the 'RaZA.' When he was once asked this question, what's the difference between philosophy and *Chassidus*, he answered: Someone who studies philosophy eventually takes off his *tzitzis* and *yarmulke*; someone who learns *Chassidus* eventually adds another hat and a *gartel* (prayer girdle).

"Personally, I have seen this clearly. Jews who studied philosophy declined in their *yiras Shamayim*. They became so smart, so intellectual, that they viewed everything through a philosophical lens. Worst of all, it damaged their *yiras Shamayim*. On the other hand, I have seen many Jews who were originally full of doubts and questions, but not long after they started to study *Chassidus*, their doubts and questions vanished and the warmth of Torah and *yiras Shamayim* started to permeate them.

"What's the source of this difference? It derives from the fundamental disparity between the two approaches. Philosophy is all about intellect and comprehension. That's the goal and purpose of philosophy, to explain everything intellectually. The fundamental approach of *Chassidus* is utterly different; its goal is not to explain, but to inject vitality, to illuminate the Jew's soul, to bring his natural faith to permeate every facet of his inner being."

"Those are quite abstract ideas, too difficult to grasp," Aharon commented. Until then he had kept quiet, but Reb Yosef Yitzchak's last words reminded him of his conversations with Elimelech.

"Since we're discussing concepts of spiritual vitality and the inner soul," Reb Yosef Yitzchak replied, "you obviously wouldn't expect me to explain all this intellectually. This is the Divine power of *P'nimius HaTorah*. It's the 'soul' of the Torah, so when one studies it, it arouses the powers of his soul.

"That's why Chassidim treat with great care the original words in which *Chassidus* was expressed by the Rebbe of each generation, because the content and explanations are only details in the study of *Chassidus*. The main point is the soul and Divine power concealed within *Chassidus*, which can be grasped specifically through the Rebbe's original words.

"In addition, discourses of *Chassidus* are full of concepts about many aspects of serving *Hashem*, inspiring us to deeper perspectives in Torah study, prayer and *mitzva*-observance with special care and feeling. That's how *Chassidus* is so different from philosophy; in fact there's no comparison whatsoever between them."

"So what will happen if I start learning *Tanya*?" Bentzion asked.

"You'll see all your questions and doubts suddenly melt away," Reb Yosef Yitzchak said. "You"ll start to disdain all the questions you used to ask; in your own eyes they'll seem embarrassing and immature. All the power they once held will vanish completely. Pure faith will begin to illuminate your soul."

"But will I also get answers to my questions?" Bentzion continued to press, grasping onto this last straw.

"In *Chassidus* you'll find the deepest answers to all questions that ever bothered you," Reb Yosef Yitzchak assured him. "But, as I said, you'll realize that isn't the main point. You'll start to study more deeply because you'll realize that the **Torah** itself expects you to understand these answers, not because you seek to remove doubts from your mind. The fact that you may not understand these matters won't bother you any more than you ever get upset by not understanding some logical point in the *Gemara*. Faith will shine within you in full force, and studying *Chassidus* will reinforce and increase your *yiras Shamayim* and desire to study the Torah. That's the Divine power of *Chassidus*. It is vitality in its innermost essence, and it endows all who study it with vitality."

CHAPTER SIXTEEN
THREE APPROACHES AND ONE MORE

Aharon was sure that the conversation with Reb Yosef Yitzchak, and his powerful negation of any involvement with intellectual philosophy, would dissuade Bentzion from ever studying it again. He was convinced his friend would now return to his old self and to his devotion to Talmud study without any distractions. Indeed, for a while it seemed that way. For Bentzion, however, the process of divesting himself of any connection with philosophy was difficult, and Aharon could discern his distress. While Bentzion now filled every hour, even his free time, with Talmud and related studies, it was obvious that his heart was not totally in it. Something was still bothering him deeply.

Yes, his decision to abandon philosophy was indeed final. He never again opened any philosophical work. His long conversations with Aharon, and particularly Reb Yosef Yitzchak's unequivocal warnings of the dangers of philosophy study, succeeded in eliminated any enthusiasm Bentzion ever had for it, together with all the justifications he had devised to defend himself and to deny the reality of spiritual decline on his part. Now he was ready to admit the truth, which is why he was determined to abandon his study of philosophy.

But those months of dabbling in philosophy had left their mark. Something had changed inside him. No longer was he the same Bentzion, for the analytical germ that had penetrated him had not left. He felt this unquenchable thirst for answers. Now he discerned all sorts of issues he had never noticed before, and his mind ceaselessly questioned, desiring to get to the bottom of everything, to understand the why and how. He could not get rid of this constant compulsion.

Aharon sensed it right away. "I think that more than providing you with answers, philosophy has taught you to ask questions," he once told him, half jokingly, yet half as a complaint.

"I don't know if that's so bad," Bentzion responded, deep in thought, as if in the midst of some dream. Indeed, he truly did not know whether it was good or bad.

"What! Do you still have some doubt?" Aharon rebuked him. "Isn't it clear to you yet how much your pure faith has been affected by your study of philosophy? Don't the negative results speak for themselves?"

"I concede that my study of philosophy was a mistake," Bentzion admitted, clearly upset. "I was absolutely in error. But I still ask: Does *Yiddishkeit* forbid asking questions? Is it really so bad to try to get to the depth of everything? Is it really prohibited to want to understand the rationale and meaning of everything?"

"I don't know why you need to ask all these questions at all," Aharon insisted. "We have one purpose in life – to study Torah, to become Torah scholars. By doing this, we also get to understand the reasons for the *mitzvos* and discover answers to all questions, because there's nothing that doesn't have an answer in the Torah. So we ought to devote ourselves entirely to Torah study, and when we possess the Torah, we will have everything."

"But what about in the meantime?" asked Bentzion.

"In the meantime we must suffice with simple faith," Aharon replied.

Bentzion heard him but could not accept it. He felt a powerful need to understand everything immediately, without delay. He was not prepared to wait for this understanding to appear some time in his old age. For many hours he pondered this, trying to marshal proofs to support each side of the argument, until finally he could express the problem in his own words, which he proceeded to share with his companion.

"When we study a *Gemara* subject, it's immediately drilled into our minds that we need to get to the bottom of the issues, to trace the source of every concept, to know the rationale behind every detail. Torah study demands of us not to let any tiny rock remain unturned: We need to delve deeply, to question, to search, to probe, until everything is understood. In other words, it's not enough to suffice with the 'body' of the subject, with the final Halachic decision, but it's demanded of us to get to its 'soul,' to the causes and sources of everything. This method of study negates an approach of just superficially reading and accepting. On the contrary, it encourages us to question and take the subject apart until everyone understands it with his own mind.

"So why is it, then," Bentzion summed up his argument, "that all these rules disappear when we talk about the essence of the Torah and *mitzvos*? Why am I told to study the Torah while no one explains in detail what's accomplished by Torah study? Why am I commanded to observe *mitzvos* without being told about their 'soul,' their reasons and spiritual meaning? Why, in this area, is it forbidden to ask questions and seek answers?"

Aharon was unimpressed. "No one negates in principle the need to understand these matters," he responded to Bentzion. "But everything has its time. First we need to study the Talmud and *Poskim* in full, and only later to study esoteric Torah subjects."

"You're making that distinction!" Bentzion protested. "From where do you get that rule? Who has determined that before we study Talmud and *Halacha* in full it's forbidden to learn and to understand why we put on *tefilin* and study Torah?"

"What's so much to know?" Aharon countered. "We put on *tefilin* because *Hashem* has commanded us, and we study Torah because that's His Will."

"If so," Bentzion snapped, "let's close our *Gemaras*. Why does the *Gemara* ask so often 'From where are these laws derived?' It should just say, 'That is our tradition we have received from our great Torah leaders, who received it from Moshe *Rabbeinu*, who heard it from *Hashem*.' Why do we need to break our minds to try to understand everything? Let's just study the simple laws in the *Mishna* and *Shulchan Aruch*, and leave the *Gemara*, with it extensive analysis and full of questions, to professional *Rabbonim* and Halachic authorities!"

"I'll tell you the difference between studying the *Gemara* and its commentaries, and studying the rationale and mystical secrets of the Torah," Aharon explained himself. "When you study a folio page of *Gemara*, you're involved in concepts close to you and your reality. It's relatively easy to understand all this because it's dealing with what's known and familiar to us. On the other hand, when you get into the realm of Torah mysticism, or, as you defined it, the meaning behind the Torah and *mitzvos*, there's a double danger involved: First, the discussion revolves around abstract, mystical concepts that are most difficult to understand properly. Second, a mistake in understanding these concepts is much more dangerous than a mistake in understanding the *Gemara* because it can easily lead one to heretical conclusions, G-d forbid. That's why I'm telling you to study such subjects only after you fully master Talmud and *Halacha*, not before."

"On that point I'm not disagreeing with you," Bentzion conceded. "But according to the way you have just presented your argument, it touches on a question of actual fact: If no safe, well-explained approach exists that teaches the Torah rationales, then you are correct that it's forbidden to touch these subjects without proper preparation. But if such an approach does exist, which avoids all the dangers you mentioned, then there's no reason not to study these subjects. On the contrary, there would even be a great advantage to doing that, because when one knows the 'soul,' then the 'body' becomes more alive. When one understands the meaning behind Torah study and *mitzvos* observance, it's much easier to fulfill them with joy and true passion."

"Do you know of such an approach? I don't." Aharon concluded the conversation. "So I don't want to hear any more about mysticism and the 'soul' of the Torah and *mitzvos*. Enough! I'm actually sick of all the discussions on these subjects. First it's Elimelech, and now you. Enough! Leave me alone."

Benzion made no reply. Actually, he was quite pleased with this conversation. The debate had enabled him to clarify the subject to himself more sharply. Now he knew more precisely the direction in which he was headed. If Aharon had looked more closely, he would have detected a sudden brightness shining in Bentzion's eyes. But he had not noticed. It was actually the mention of Elimelech's name that had kindled the spark.

**

It was a cloudy, rainy night when Bentzion knocked at Reb Yosef Yitzchak's door. The warmth with which Reb Yosef Yitzchak had welcomed them last time encouraged him to return. Once again he intuitively felt this was the person with whom he could discuss what troubled him. This time, however, he decided to come alone, without Aharon or Elimelech.

Reb Yosef Yitzchak opened the door with astonishment. He had not expected this visit. When Bentzion had sat there last time, Reb Yosef Yitzchak had been seriously concerned about him. He was familiar with this type of yeshiva student, and knew well that if he got involved with intellectual philosophy, it could cause inestimable harm to the student's *yiras Shamayim* and commitment to Torah study and observance of *mitzvos*.

At that previous meeting, Reb Yosef Yitzchak had been in a difficult position. While sharply negating involvement in philosophy, he had not emphasized with equal force an alternate solution. Only delicately had he suggested that *Chassidus* study would satisfy what Bentzion sought and would strengthen his faith. But he was not so naive to assume that Bentzion would start studying *Chassidus* the next morning. So it was with great satisfaction that he saw Bentzion apparently had digested his subtle message.

Bentzion amazed Reb Yosef Yitzchak with the free and open way he shared his turmoil and the problem that had been bothering him. He was happy to repeat the arguments he had offered to Aharon, that just as one studies the 'body of the Torah, so should one study its 'soul,' too. Now he sought to know what were the various approaches in *Yiddishkeit* for studying the 'soul' of the Torah and *mitzvos*.

"If you're asking what is the 'soul' of the Torah," Reb Yosef Yitzchak began, "the answer is simple. The Torah has been given to us on two levels, one hidden, *Nistar*, and one revealed, *Nigleh*. Talmud and *Halacha* constitute *Nigleh*, and *Nistar* is *P'nimius HaTorah*, the inner dimension of the Torah, as revealed in the *Kabbala* and mysticism. The *Zohar*, the central work of the *Kabbala*, states that *Nigleh* is the 'body' of the Torah, while *Nistar* is its 'soul.'

"That's the short answer to your question. But it's worthwhile for you to know the subject from a broader perspective. Actually, alongside study of Talmud and *Halacha*, there have always existed various approaches aiming to inspire us to serve *Hashem* better, to arouse love and awe of Him, to rid ourselves of undesirable traits, etc. These, too, are integral parts of the Torah and need to be studied.

"In general, there are three approaches: a) *mussar*, b) *chakira*, philosophy, and c) *Kabbala*. Each of these is a path for serving *Hashem* and worthy of study on its own. Throughout the generations, hundreds of thousands of Jews have become adherents of one or another of these paths. Each has an advantage not possessed by the others. But each also has a drawback the others don't have, which is why many have followed one or another of these approaches while rejecting the others.

"*Mussar*'s advantage is that it deals with the person directly, with his character and inner essence. The approach of *mussar* explains the nature of one's character traits and various tendencies, and gives guidance how to overcome and eliminate those negative traits, and to implant positive, noble qualities instead.

"*Mussar*'s drawback is expressed in the saying, 'One who wrestles with a filthy person becomes filthy himself.' The goal is obviously holy and true, but it forces one to become involved with his negative traits and murky inclinations, with all the negativity within him. True, sometimes it's necessary to roll up your sleeves and remove the dirt piling up in your home. But removing dirt inevitably leads to soiling yourself in the process. The constant focus on evil and negative traits, on penetrating to their depths and involvement with them, envelops one in melancholy and causes constant depression.

"The approach of *chakira* is in utter contrast to that of *mussar*. It holds that there's no need to be involved with evil, preferring instead that we become attached to exalted and uplifting concepts, based on the premise that light automatically removes darkness. Accordingly, Jewish philosophy encourages delving into the secrets of creation, into the rationale for the Torah and *mitzvos*, and the exalted greatness of *Hashem*, etc. By becoming devoted to such exalted concepts, we sense how foolish and worthless it is to be devoted to base desires and evil traits. The light drives away the evil, which just fades away on its own.

"This approach has another advantage over *mussar*. Both have the same goal, to remove evil traits and develop good ones, and to become devoted to the Torah and serving *Hashem*. It may happen, however, that one does not succeed in reaching that goal. He studies, reflects, meditates, but fails to change his essential nature. And here the great difference between these two approaches is most pronounced: One who has been involved with *mussar*, but has failed, with what is he left? He has been plunged into dirt and dark character! But if he has been involved in lofty, exalted concepts, what has been his focus? In great and holy concepts! Someone walking out of a perfume store gives off a pleasant fragrance; likewise one who has been involved in uplifting concepts, whatever happens, he becomes automatically uplifted.

"That's philosophy's advantage over *mussar*. But it also has a drawback, which you've already heard from me last time you were here: Philosophy is a purely intellectual pursuit. One relates to everything with limited human intelligence alone, which can easily cause his faith to become concealed and lost. When the whole approach is intellectual and analytical, it raises many questions and challenges, for which definitive answers may not be found, thereby undermining one's faith. That's why many great Torah leaders prohibited, even sharply, any study of philosophy.

"The third approach is *Kabbala*. This discipline, too, involves uplifting, exalted concepts, which is why it is more similar to philosophy than to *mussar*. But *Kabbala*'s style is not intellectual or analytical. *Kabbala* means 'receiving,' and that's what it is, a received tradition, passed from master to disciple. Intellect is not what is most important here, and questions and answers are not what define its concepts. In *Kabbala* one listens and accepts, comes to know and understand. Anyone who studies *Kabbala* realizes it's not an open area of study in which anyone can innovate or wander about with his intellect as he desires. Study of *Kabbala* is enveloped in and permeated with holiness and purity, which is why the risks inherent in study of philosophy are entirely avoided in this approach."

"Does *Kabbala*, too, have a drawback?" asked Bentzion, anticipating the next point.

"Correct," smiled Reb Yosef Yitzchak. "It's a fact that many great Torah leaders tended to avoid study of *Kabbala*, for good reason. *Kabbala*'s drawback is that it teaches about concepts so refined and abstract, but often describes them in terms and with names that sound physical, which makes them easy to misinterpret when those without full knowledge and awareness do not know how to divest the concepts of their outer, physical-sounding façade. Thus there is a serious concern of ascribing physical qualities to exalted spiritual concepts, or making other serious errors regarding such holy, sensitive concepts. That's why many fine Jews were careful not to approach *Kabbala* until they had first studied Talmud and *Halacha* to the fullest extent, and had prepared themselves properly in the spiritual sense."

"What a conundrum!" Bentzion mused aloud. He was fascinated by the way Reb Yosef Yitzchak so clearly expounded the world of Jewish thought, outlining the various approaches with the advantages and disadvantages of each. When Reb Yosef Yitzchak described the advantages of each approach, Bentzion had been so excited. But then he felt deeply disappointed to hear of its drawbacks. Now this whole dilemma seemed too difficult to resolve.

"You're right, it is a conundrum, to some degree," Reb Yosef Yitzchak agreed. "That's why there have always been Jews who preferred the risks of one approach or the other and claimed that its advantages were greater than its risks. Nevertheless, we have never felt completely safe.

"There is, however, one further approach that combines the advantages of all three approaches, without any of their drawbacks. It refines and purifies our character traits, with no need to wrestle with them or to become soiled by dealing with them directly. It also explains concepts logically so that we can understand them, without the danger of intellect becoming dominant, without the analytical emphasis that can be so harmful. And it's based entirely on the holy *Kabbala*, but its explanations and its development of those abstract concepts circumvent all the concerns associated with *Kabbala* study."

"That must be *Chassidus*!" Bentzion guessed.

"Yes, it's *Chassidus*," Reb Yosef Yitzchak confirmed. "It's the great revelation by the Baal Shem Tov and his holy disciples, especially as explained and expanded through the approach of *Chassidus* Chabad."

For a long time they both sat silently, deep in thought. Suddenly Bentzion roused himself and glanced at his watch. Shocked at how late it was, he mumbled a quick thanks and left Reb Yosef Yitzchak's home without another word.

CHAPTER SEVENTEEN
THERE'S A SOUL!

Bentzion was not the hesitating type who suffered from indecision. He had always been quite daring, almost impetuous. When he reached some conclusion, as strange or unacceptable as it might seem, he would not hesitate for a moment to act on it. Others' opinions were the last thing he took into consideration. That was how, later that week after meeting Reb Yosef Yitzchak for the second time, he was already sitting with Elimelech to study *Tanya*.

That week he tried several times to get accepted into Reb Yosef Yitzchak's class. But Reb Yosef Yitzchak considered the class to have enough students and refused to accept any more, directing new applicants to wait until enough students applied before a new class would be started. But Bentzion was not one to wait around patiently. Determined to achieve his goal as soon as possible, he exerted some effort to convince Elimelech to give him his own private *Tanya* lesson. Elimelech emphasized repeatedly that he himself was just a beginner, but Bentzion told him, "That's enough for me!"

They began to study twice a week, meeting after the end of the evening study sessions at their yeshivos. Elimelech had just one request: "Let's not talk about *Chassidus*. Let's study it, spending less time on defining the nature of the 'water,' but drinking it instead!"

Bentzion agreed wholeheartedly.

Already in their first study sessions, Bentzion realized how deep was Elimelech's grasp of the subject matter. He already swam freely in the sea of *Chassidus* with confidence, like an experienced regular. Often he would respond to a question of Bentzion by telling him he did not know the answer, but it was obvious he had developed such a clear, definitive approach to *Chassidus* study that it was a pleasure to study with him.

Bentzion was not surprised, for he remembered how talented Elimelech was from when they had studied together in the *yeshiva ketana*. What really amazed him, though, was Elimelech's energy, the way he lived and breathed what he studied. Even when his friend did not state it verbally, he sensed how his friend found practical application in every line and concept in *Tanya*. He did not approach what he studied as something theoretical but as the reality in a Jew's everyday life in this world. The way Elimelech actually "lived" the concepts of *Chassidus* astounded him.

For himself, however, Bentzion sought something else in studying *Chassidus*. He yearned to discover secrets, to comprehend the world in a deeper manner, with intellectual understanding. In contrast, Elimelech sought a way of life and guidance in serving *Hashem*. So even with all his admiration for his friend, Bentzion was somewhat confused at first by Elimelech's differing emphasis and by his excited reaction to what often seemed trivial to Bentzion.

On the other hand, his own enthusiasm grew whenever he was introduced to an idea that totally shattered all his previous notions, opening his eyes to an inner, more profound perspective. That was when he would get so excited that his heart would sing within him.

The end of *Tanya*'s first chapter, and then the second chapter, left him open-mouthed, giving him food for thought for many days. It was like a flash of light that in single moment illuminated his entire world outlook. For the first time in his life, he grasped what the term "soul" meant, especially the Jewish soul.

Until then, his conception of a soul had been very vague. Sure, there was something called a soul, a sort of spiritual spark, abstract and indefinable – that's what he would think of whenever the term came up from time to time. He also knew there was some sort of connection between himself and that spark called the 'soul.' Obviously, it was his spark, his soul. He knew he was obligated to study Torah and fulfill the *mitzvos* so that, after 120 years, this spark, his soul, would go to Paradise and not to the opposite place. Actually, more than once he had wondered what exactly he would gain from this spark getting to Paradise. And then he would berate himself and think how foolish were those ideas falling into his mind; when the soul will be privileged to enter *Gan Eden*, he too would benefit! But he did not actually understand the nature of the connection between himself and his soul.

From the viewpoint of what was happening within himself, he knew there was a *yetzer tov* and a *yetzer hara*, and that the two battled ceaselessly. In his mind, he imagined them as two little advisors sending him various ideas from time to time, which was when he had to mediate between them to decide how to act.

Suddenly, in *Tanya*, he discovered an entirely different world.

First of all, there are no two little advisors but two actual souls enlivening him and functioning within him. He learned that a soul means the life-force of something, the spirit of life that enlivens its essence. Also he learned that the soul is the basic aspect of every being, that when something is said to be its soul, it means it is everything, for every being's essence is its soul.

Thus, when it is said that a Jew has two souls, a Divine soul and an animal soul, it means that a Jew's entire essence is that combination, or the struggle between those two souls. Suddenly he grasped that when he referred to himself as "I," what he actually meant was the composite of these two souls: "I" is the relationship between the Divine soul and the animal soul.

When Elimelech began to explain this concept, Bentzion did not at first understand why he found it so important to emphasize that the soul is the basis and entirety of every being, and would also speak about spirituality as being the basis of everything.

Suddenly, as if a beam of light penetrated his mind, the implications of this concept wrought a radical change in his mind. He began to realize how these were not theoretical concepts or just symbols, but something very real, just like his thoughts and feelings. His recognition that his soul was his "I" became so crystal clear, and this excited him immensely.

Later, Bentzion liked to relate how, until that moment, his soul had hovered somewhere in the seventh heaven, and then, suddenly, it had entered and become part of him. Not only did it become part of him, but it became his entire self and essence.

Another point that struck him with wonder was *Tanya's* explanation, at the end of Chapter 1, of the difference between a

Jew and a gentile. It gave an entirely new meaning to the word "Jew" and what was meant when one said "I am a Jew."

He learned that the common denominator between Jew and gentile is that a Jew's animal soul and a gentile's soul both derive from the realm of *klipa*, the veneer concealing the true Divine essence of the universe.

But the difference between them is that a gentile's soul derives from *klipos* that utterly conceal the Divine holiness and therefore contain nothing positive, as the *Gemara* (*Bava Basra* 10b) comments on the verse (*Mishlei* 14:34), "The kindness of nations is sinful" – "All charity and kindness of the nations are only for their own prestige." But the Jew's animal soul, although it too derives from *klipa*, it is a *klipa* that has some good mixed into it, which is why, besides its innate evil traits, it also possesses good qualities natural to every Jew – compassion, kindness and bashfulness (as the *Gemara* says in *Yevamos* 79a).

This idea utterly amazed Bentzion. Such a concept had never occurred to him. These positive qualities that distinguish the Jewish people, which are the clear indication of one's Jewishness to the extent that our Sages say that anyone without these three qualities is not worthy of marrying into the Jewish people – to think that these are expressions of the animal soul, which derives from *klipa*, and to think that the Jew's animal soul is naturally compassionate and kind!

The obvious conclusion then is – and that is what sprang out of his mouth as if of its own accord – if this is the animal soul, then how much greater must be the Divine soul!

"We'll learn about the Divine soul in Chapter 2 of *Tanya*," Elimelech told him.

During those few days between studying the end of Chapter 1 and beginning Chapter 2, Bentzion walked around in a state of overwhelming excitement. Slowly he started to realize that, without studying *Chassidus*, one has no way to judge the true order of everything's greatness. Someone previously considered, according to the ordinary conception of the term, to be a perfect *tzaddik*, is suddenly revealed as not having reached even the level of a *beinoni*, the "intermediate" level. Positive character traits once considered to be the height of the *yetzer tov*'s perfection are understood as merely natural traits of the animal soul.

He once mentioned this astonishing revelation to Elimelech, who agreed with him completely. Indeed, Elimelech added, without studying *Chassidus*, one floats through life most likely with false ideas and delusions without any conception of the true essence of everything.

Those days that passed between study of the end of Chapter 1 of *Tanya* and Chapter 2 were a time of deep thought and reflection for Bentzion. For the first time ever, he felt he had the tools for understanding the world. His thoughts speeded ahead, trying to embrace and grasp other implications that might be deduced from what he had learned. Above all, an intense yearning to study *Tanya*, Chapter 2, beat within him. He had never felt such a thirst and yearning. Now that he knew he had a soul within him, he desperately wanted to know what it was...

One word explained everything. Chapter 2 opened with the

words, "And the second soul in the Jew is a part of G-d from Above, literally." Elimelech pointed to the added word "literally," repeating it several times: "'Literally,' just as it says; a part of *Hashem* from Above, literally. The Divine soul within every Jew is a part of G-d, literally a part of *Hashem*!"

Bentzion needed a few moments to digest this revolutionary idea. But Elimelech ignored his difficulty in grasping it and proceeded to explain the following lines of the chapter. He explained, with relatively broad elaboration, the meaning of the verse, "and He blew into his nostrils a living soul," which refers to the creation of Adam *Harishon*. This word "blew," he explained, is a metaphor used to convey the idea that just as, when someone blows on the physical level, he forces energy from deep within him to reach what he is blowing at, so it is in the creation of the human being, that his life-force derives from *Hashem*'s very essence. With these words, then, the Torah teaches that, when creating the human being, the innermost essence of He who blew, *Hashem*, was infused into Adam.

Bentzion was still in a haze, but Elimelech continued. The next few lines clarified the meaning of the expression "a part of G-d" in terms of its source, and removed any doubt that the phrase was referring to anything but a literal "part of G-d," part of *Hashem*'s Divine Oneness. Here Elimelech stopped to develop and elucidate the subject.

"The Divine soul," he explained, "is not some spiritual being like an angel, nor even a reflection of Divine light. This soul is a part of *Hashem*, of His very essence. Such a part of *Hashem* exists within me and within you. It's my inner essential self, and yours too, and every Jew's."

They continued no further in *Tanya* that evening. Instead they sat together until late, trying better to understand the meaning of this new revelation. Gradually, it began to penetrate Bentzion's mind that a part of *Hashem* actually existed within him, "a part of G-d from Above, literally." He started to realize that his soul was not somewhere in Heaven or concealed deep within his body. He realized that the soul was not some vague spark but was his entire inner essence, his true "I"!

Now he understood the meaning of an "arousal of *teshuva*," and of our Sages' teaching that the soul hears a Heavenly voice which emerges every day, and it thereby becomes aroused. The soul means "I myself." When the soul is aroused, it means that something within me is stirred, it demands and searches. It's not something distant but something inside me, within me.

His whole being sang out joyfully, "I have a Divine Soul! I have within me 'a part of G-d from Above, literally'!" He sensed that this was not something describable in words or by using intellect. The words themselves had never changed — "soul," "Divine soul." But now, for the first time, he understood their true meaning.

Their deep discussion gradually drifted from the theoretical level to its practical implications. Elimelech explained that the perspective outlined in these chapters of Tanya led to other profound ideas regarding the relationship of one Jew to another, and gave new meaning to the concept of *ahavas Yisroel*, love of fellow Jews. With these concepts, there is what to love and whom to love. When one reflects on this, that every Jew, no difference who he is, has a Divine soul, how could one not love his fellow?

"From here derives the Chassidic love of every Jew," Elimelech told Bentzion. "That's why *Chassidus* is distinguished by its *ahavas Yisroel* and its activity on behalf of every Jew, whoever it is. *Chassidus* teaches us to see the essential soul within every Jew, and the natural result of this is to love that Jew truly."

When Bentzion got back to his yeshiva, he did not go to sleep, despite the late hour. He entered the mostly darkened study hall, sat in a corner, and opened the *Tanya* he kept in his pocket. He felt compelled to review those lines again and to think them over one more time.

He reflected on what Elimelech had said on reading the words near the end of Chapter 1: "Every Jewish person, whether he is righteous or wicked, has two souls." The meaning was clear – in the inner essence of the Jew there was no difference between one who is called wicked, who does not study Torah or observe *mitzvos*, and someone who studies Torah day and night and fulfills every *mitzva*, major or minor, with special care and devotion. Both of them equally have the same two souls, a Divine soul and an animal soul. In their essence there is no difference between them. Any difference exists only in how much success the Divine soul has in overcoming the animal soul. Yet even when a Divine soul succeeds in triumphing fully over the animal soul, there is still no change in his inner essence.

The high ladder of hierarchy once firmly established in his mind now collapsed and vanished before his eyes as he recognized this truth. Status does not exist, and there are no two types of Jews on differing levels. There are just two souls, the Divine soul and the animal soul, the same two for both the wicked and the righteous alike. This was a radically innovative concept for him.

But that was only one side of the story. He turned to its other implication, the difference between Jew and gentile. Until he studied the end of Chapter 1 in *Tanya*, it had never occurred to him that there was any essential difference between them. Later, Bentzion would describe his previous outlook as paradoxical, without his ever having noticed it. On the one hand, it was clear to him that someone devoted to Torah study had a unique status and stood on a pedestal of prestige. On the other hand, the difference between Jew and gentile was not so clear. Within the Jewish nation he saw divisions, but the division between Jew and gentile was vague.

It was specifically his realization of the non-existence of a caste system among the Jewish people, and his recognition of the essential unity of all Jews, that led to a sharper sense of the essential difference between Jews and gentiles. Bentzion would later say that, although superficially the two concepts would seem to constitute a paradox, serious examination would show that not only were they not contradictary but that the two ideas were intricately connected.

Chassidus brought him to relate to spiritual concepts just as he related to physical reality. He came to realize that the soul exists just as a body exists, and that the difference between Jew and gentile is essential. Just as *Hashem* differentiated between light and darkness, so does He differentiate between Jews and other nations. Until then, spirituality had been an abstract concept, not at all real. Now spirituality had become palpable and actual to him, it existed in reality just like physical beings and objects.

Bentzion sat, spellbound, for a long time, not noticing how much time he spent in the empty study hall. Eventually, far into the night, he went to his room, where he found Aharon sleeping deeply. He prevented himself from the temptation to wake him, despite his deep desire to tell him, "Aharon, without *Chassidus* you're like a blind man groping in the dark. Start studying *Chassidus* and your eyes will be opened!" As he recalled his friend's fears of mysticism and concepts he could not understood, he whispered, "Aharon, if only you, too, would experience this exalted light!"

CHAPTER EIGHTEEN
"MY SOUL THIRSTS FOR YOU, *HASHEM*"

One Thursday evening, after the *Tanya* class ended, Reb Yosef Yitzchak motioned to Elimelech that he wanted to speak to him on his own. Elimelech had no idea what it was about.

Reb Yosef Yitzchak did not start right away. He seemed to be thinking how to tell him something important, trying to choose his words carefully.

"Elimelech, you've already gained wide knowledge of *Chassidus*. You've learned many chapters of *Tanya* and studied a number of Chassidic discourses. You're well familiar with many concepts. I think it's time for you to start to *daven*."

"What do you mean, to *daven*?" Elimelech was bewildered. "Don't I already pray three times a day?" It took him a while to digest this unexpected statement.

"Surely you've learned enough *Chassidus* to understand what *davenen* really means," Reb Yosef Yitzchak looked him in the eyes intently. "It's time for you to begin to get into *avodas hatefila*, serving *Hashem* through prayer, to pray according to the special way that *Chassidus* views prayer."

"Actually, although I've often seen it mentioned in *Chassidus*, I really don't know what it means in practice," said Elimelech.

"Don't worry," Reb Yosef Yitzchak reassured him. "That's why I want to discuss it with you. But before I explain what *avodas hatefila* is, let's first review what you already know about it."

"I know that *Chassidus* places great emphasis on connecting with *Hashem* through prayer," said Elimelech. "That's in addition to the basic obligation of prayer – to ask for our needs, which is the usual view of prayer without the additional illumination of *Chassidus*."

"Good," said Reb Yosef Yitzchak. "You have the basic idea. But there are many details in connecting with *Hashem* through prayer, and it's accomplished through *avodas hatefila*.

"Throughout the day, we study *Nigleh* and *Chassidus*, and observe *mitzvos*. This aspect of our spiritual *avoda* can be compared to mixing flour, water and other ingredients to prepare for baking them into bread. But mixing all the ingredients alone is obviously not enough. After all that, they have to undergo a process of baking which transforms them into a complete final product. This is accomplished by prayer.

"When we pray, what we have studied in *Chassidus*, together with all our positive resolutions to refine ourselves based on that study, becomes firmly established within us. Prayer enables us to crush and remove our negative aspects. This is accomplished through our passion in prayer and the inspiration it arouses. We become attached to the subject of our deep meditation on *Hashem*'s greatness and to the Divine light shining through our words of prayer."

"How is that accomplished?" Elimelech wondered. "How can all my personal affairs be connected with my prayers? Aren't we supposed to think what the words mean when we pray?"

"True," Reb Yosef Yitzchak agreed. "The meaning of the words is the basis of everything in prayer. But *Chassidus* teaches us how to find, in the words of our prayers, the fundamentals of meditation connected with our service of *Hashem*.

"Within this, too, there are levels. On starting *avodas hatefila*, one needs to focus mainly on the meaning of the words and to learn the spiritual content of every verse in our prayers, as explained in *Chassidus*. At a further stage, one can start meditation.

"As far as you're concerned, I'm referring to the simplest level of *avodas hatefila* – to pray passionately while thinking about the meaning of the words. This is something very important for you to do."

"Am I ready for this? Does this special *avoda* apply to me at my level?" Elimelech asked doubtfully. The concept seemed far beyond his reach.

"Absolutely!" Reb Yosef Yitzchak insisted. "It applies to everyone. We're not talking about some lofty ideal applying only to those of high spiritual level. This is an *avoda* that every Jew needs to do, because it's necessary for everyone. Everyone prays, and everyone needs to know how to pray. In particular, your character and spiritual inclinations are those of an *oved*, the term Chassidim use to refer to someone who works on his inner character, and it would be a pity not to direct your inclinations in the right direction."

Overwhelmed, Elimelech did not respond. It all sounded somewhat vague. He realized that something great and important was being demanded of him, but was not quite sure what it was, or how he was supposed to do it. The thoughts raced through his mind incoherently, and he had a hard time focusing and organizing his feelings.

Reb Yosef Yitchok understood that Elimelech would need a few moments to digest what he had told him, so he waited until he succeeded in pulling himself together.

"So what exactly am I supposed to do?" Elimelech finally asked.

"I suggest you start your *avodas hatefila* every *Shabbos*," said Reb Yosef Yitzchak. "This *Shabbos*, start to pray all the prayers according to *Chassidus*."

"Will it take a lot of time? Will I still be able to pray along with the *minyan*?" asked Elimelech.

"I don't know how much time you'll need," Reb Yosef Yitzchak told him. "It's very personal. But there's no reason to assume you won't be able to pray with the *minyan*. If you find the *minyan* is praying too fast, you can simply start your prayers half an hour earlier. Initially at least, try to pray along with the *minyan*, at the same pace."

"So what will I actually be doing?" Elimelech asked.

"You choose a chapter of *Tanya* or a discourse of *Chassidus* which you feel, when you study it, that it really touches your heart and affects you deeply," Reb Yosef Yitzchak explained. "You should study that chapter or discourse until you know it very well, by heart, whether word by word (especially if it's a chapter of *Tanya*), or at least the content in its original order, whatever you find has most impact on you. Obviously, you'll need to understand all its details well. All that should be done before you start your actual preparation for prayer."

"What do you mean, 'preparation for prayer'? Is preparation also required before prayer?" Elimelech asked, feeling that perhaps there was much more to find out about this whole process.

"Of course," Reb Yosef Yitzchak confirmed. "Do you think you can jump straight out of your pajamas into standing before *Hashem*? Our Sages say, 'One should stand up to pray only from solemnity,' which Rashi explains to mean 'humility.' We need to humble ourselves before we can approach prayer. As long as we still feel our ego and our own wishes and desires, how can we connect with *Hashem*?

"That's why Chassidim immerse themselves in a *mikva* before prayer. Besides purifying both body and soul, immersion also humbles and 'nullifies' one. *Kabbala* and *Chassidus* explain that this connection is expressed in the very letters of the word *TeViLaH* – Hebrew for "immersion" – which, rearranged, are the same as those of *HaBiTuL* – "nullification" and humility.

"But immersion in a *mikva*, on its own, is not enough. There must also be an inner soul preparation, which is why, before we pray, we study *Chassidus*, where we learn about *Hashem*'s greatness, about the connection between a Jew's soul and *Hashem*, etc. This study humbles us and prepares us for prayer."

"What should one meditate about?" Elimelech now asked. He was starting to sense how much his heart was drawn to this. The description he had heard about preparation for prayer gave it a far deeper dimension. It seemed so straightforward to understand, as if it couldn't be different, yet all this had never occurred to him.

"You take the chapter of *Tanya* or discourse of *Chassidus* that you've already studied well and that has excited you," Reb Yosef Yitzchak explained. "That is now your subject of meditation. Meditation doesn't mean just reviewing it in your mind. It means looking within, penetrating to the concept's deeper meaning and implications. Of course, when you study, too, you need to meditate on the subject, but it's a different meditation from the meditation before and in prayer. Meditation in Torah study has the goal of understanding the subject better, while the meditation of prayer is to arouse feeling, to sense what it's telling you. Its goal is to try to feel the Divine in the concept so that it shines within your soul.

"For now, I can't give any more details. Just start to pray and you'll discover on your own how to meditate and how to feel the G-dly light of *Chassidus*."

"What about the prayer itself?" Elimelech asked. "Do I pray differently from the way I've been doing it till now?"

Slowly he was beginning to see that it might not be so complicated after all.

"Pray slowly, your ears hearing every word you utter, and try to pay attention to the words' meaning," Reb Yosef Yitzchak answered. "But be careful to avoid any superficiality. Don't make conspicuous movements. Try to ensure no one can tell you're doing anything special or different. This *avoda* is internal, within you, and is not expressed outwardly. If you pray properly, your heart will be aroused on its own. You're speaking to *Hashem*, not playing with emotions. Prayer is not an 'experience'; it's hard work. The *Zohar* says that 'The time of prayer is a time of battle.' That's how you should relate to prayer.

"Just start. And avoid conspicuousness. Nothing should be noticeable from the outside."

***

All the amazing stories and exalted descriptions of prayer in general, and particularly the way great Chassidim had prayed, came to Elimelech's mind. He recalled how fascinated he had been by what Reb Yosef Yitzchak had related and by stories he had read about how Chassidim prayed with all their soul. He too had longed to leave his bounds and to merge within *Hashem*'s light, but he realized how far he was from that. And now Reb Yosef Yitzchak was directing him to enter that world of prayer.

One story he remembered was of a *Chassid* too exhausted one night to study any more Torah. He had gone over to the sink to wash his hands in order to recite the prayers of night-time *Sh'ma* before sleep. As he stood by the sink, he had fallen into meditation on a deep concept of *Chassidus*, and remained in that state until the sun rose!

Elimelech was especially moved by the story of a *Chassid* so affected by the *Yom Kippur* prayers that, even after the fast day had ended, he remained in *shul*, dancing around the Torah-reading desk as he sang to a soulful melody the mystical poem of Divine unity, the *Shir Hayichud* that starts *An'im Z'miros* – including the words, "Because my soul longs for You... to know all Your secrets..." So deeply did he meditate that he did not notice the hours passing until dawn, when Jews came to *shul* for the morning prayers and found him dancing and singing!

Another fascinating story that had impressed him deeply was recorded in rich detail by the Rebbe RaYYaTz: Reb Yosef was a Torah scholar and outstanding *Chassid*, who taught many students. Once, the Alter Rebbe instructed him, strangely, to become a wagon driver. As difficult as it was, he obeyed his Rebbe's directive. This continued until once he stayed overnight in the same inn as a Jew who had fallen from Torah observance. When that Jew heard Reb Yosef's prayer, pouring out his heart for many hours, he burst into tears and became aroused to complete *teshuva*. Soon after, the Alter Rebbe's son and successor told Reb Yosef that he had thereby fulfilled the entire purpose of his becoming a wagon driver and now he could become a *Mashpia*!

These stories and others, as much as they fascinated and excited him, made him realize how, in comparison to the *avodas hatefila* of these exalted Chassidim, his own level of prayer was so low and minimal. Not all those Chassidim were necessarily great intellectual geniuses possessing lofty souls. Indeed, many were relatively unlearned, even simple, but they served *Hashem* on a level he could not even fathom. One, for example, was a simple *Chassid* who prayed for forty years with a saying of the Alter Rebbe on the words of our Sages about the two Scriptural versions of the fourth of the Ten Commandments, "'Keep' and 'Remember' [were said] in one utterance" – "In every single utterance [that we say], we should remember and keep the One [*Hashem*'s unity]."

***

Elimelech for long remembered his first attempts at *avodas hatefila*. When he sat down in his place long before the prayers were due to start, he began to meditate on a *Chassidus* text, and then started praying before anyone arrived. Throughout, he was sure everyone who happened to enter the study hall was staring at him. Noticing another student passing nearby, he was sure he was looking at him strangely and passing by expressly to watch him. It took Elimelech a long time before he succeeded in liberating himself from his self-conscious tension to focus exclusively on his prayer.

When he first started to meditate, he realized how much effort it demanded to maintain continuous mental focus on a concept. It had never occurred to him he would need to muster such powerful self-control to prevent his mind from wandering. This never happened to him during Torah study when, with minimal effort, he usually succeeded in maintaining a clear train of thought without his mind going off on tangents. Only when he meditated on a subject of *Chassidus* before prayer, did it seem that the *yetzer hara* suddenly appeared to make his thoughts run like sand though his fingers! It took a process lasting for weeks until, slowly but surely, he managed to control his thoughts for a short moment, then another and another, until he was able to meditate on a complete concept without drifting from it.

Despite Reb Yosef Yitzchak's warnings not to expect a special experience or to anticipate obscure emotions, Elimelech found himself hoping for them. He knew that *avodas hatefila* was hard work, not some exciting adventure, but still he wished to feel something in his heart, some uplifting inspiration. So at first he felt frustrated and wondered where the feelings were, why he felt no more than waves of emotion without any direction. He wished for prayer to uplift his soul, to leave a spiritual impression that would last all week, but it did not happen.

Reb Yosef Yitzchak had to spend much time explaining to him

the correct process of *avodas hatefila*, until Elimelech was finally convinced that authentic emotion could not be achieved so easily, and that every significant, fundamental change could come only through hard toil. "Prayer is not hocus-pocus magic," he told Elimelech. "You can't just press a button and suddenly become a different person. The animal soul and the body are not easily refined. Don't expect immediate success; don't bother thinking of success in the first place. You just need to work, to be involved in prayer, and the result will come on its own if you don't think about it."

Despite Elimelech's best efforts, it was hard to let go of the habit of conspicuous external movements during prayer. He really needed to see living examples of others praying properly in order to discern the difference between authenticity and superficiality. That is how he came to spend a *Shabbos* in *Yeshivas Tom'chei T'mimim*.

CHAPTER NINETEEN
THE WORLD OF THE *T'MIMIM*

Elimelech stood before the entrance of *Yeshivas Tom'chei T'mimim* in *Kfar Chabad*, scanning the faces of the students passing by. For long he had been impressed by the special look on Lubavitcher students' faces – a sense of purity and joy, something he could not exactly define. Clearly these students were immersed in a different world, a world truer and more exalted than that with which he was familiar.

On the one hand, he was overjoyed finally to be visiting *Tom'chei T'mimim*, about which he had heard so much and where he hoped to see live models of everything Reb Yosef Yitzchak had told him and about which he had studied in *Chassidus*. On the other hand, he hoped not to be disappointed by discovering that all the exalted descriptions of *Tom'chei T'mimim* had been exaggerated or only reflected some distant past. In fact, he did not quite believe all he had heard to be really true.

The bus he had taken to *Kfar Chabad* had been full of *T'mimim* students returning from Tel Aviv, where they had been busy doing *mivtzo'im* – *mitzva* campaigns, especially helping Jews fulfill the *mitzva* of *tefilin* at various locations in the city. That was how they spent every Friday afternoon after their study session ended around midday.

Elimelech regarded Tel Aviv as did most students of other yeshivos – with a feeling of disgust at the blatant immodesty prevailing there. So he was curious to learn how it affected the

Chabad students who did *mivtzo'im* there, and was interested in hearing their conversations as they returned by bus after spending several hours in the city's hustle and bustle.

He had heard about it before but, when he saw it in real time, he could not help but be impressed. All these students not only looked but also acted like Chassidic young men, with unimpaired *yiras Shamayim*. Some were holding *Chumashim* to recite the weekly Torah portion, as *Shulchan Aruch* requires on Friday – each verse of the *Chumash* twice, followed by its Aramaic translation, *Targum Onkelos*. Others were reading various booklets of the Lubavitcher Rebbe's *sichos*. Yet others were chatting, but it was not empty talk. The conversation of two students behind him sounded at first like small talk, but it was actually full of serious content. They started with the latest news from 770, the Chabad world center in Crown Heights, New York, where the Rebbe lived and prayed and *farbreng*ed. Then they discussed their latest *farbrengen* at the yeshiva, before turning to methods of outreach in various *mivtzo'im*, then brainstorming on how to attract a certain yeshiva student closer to *Chassidus*. He was amazed how their small talk and that of other students he overheard was full of holiness and Chassidic spirit.

These students were clearly not influenced by the secular atmosphere of the streets where they had just spent several hours. Indeed, they were clearly reinforced and invigorated from having positively impacted the Jews with whom they had come in contact and whom they had given an opportunity to fulfill *mitzvos*.

Elimelech recalled an anecdote Reb Yosef Yitzchak had shared of a father who explained why he had sent his son to *Tom'chei T'mimim*: "I can send him to other yeshivos, too, to learn complicated *sugyos*, but I prefer to send him to *Tom'chei T'mimim* for their small talk, because that kind of 'idle' conversation can't be found in any other yeshiva!"

***

As *Shabbos* began, all the students prayed *Mincha* together. Elimelech expected them soon to start the *Kabbolas Shabbos* prayers. Instead, he was surprised to see all the students sitting down in pairs, and starting to study books of *Chassidus*. Before Elimelech could ask any questions, a student assigned to guide him through the *Shabbos* told him he was going to bring a couple of books to study together.

"Why is there a study session now before *Kabbolas Shabbos*, and not after the *Shabbos* meal?" asked Elimelech when the student returned.

"After the meal there would no longer be much benefit to our study," the student replied with a smile. "The whole point of this session is to prepare us for the *Shabbos* evening prayers. It's not primarily for the purpose of gaining knowledge of *Chassidus*. It's a preparation for prayer so that we can pray more devoutly. After the meal, what would be the point?"

Gradually the meaning of *Shabbos* in *Tom'chei T'mimim* dawned on Elimelech. Suddenly *Shabbos* gained special significance even for him as a Torah student. Until then he had never understood the importance *Shabbos* held for him. For a Torah student, what is the difference between *Shabbos* and a weekday? During the week he is not working and is immersed in the world of Torah and serving *Hashem*, so there is nothing to distract him. If so, what is so special for him about *Shabbos*? Studying Torah was what he did all week, every day and on *Shabbos*. Of course, a businessman or employee, involved all week in mundane activities, can rise up on *Shabbos* to a world of Torah and holiness. But what is special about *Shabbos* for Torah students, for whom it is just another day to study Torah and pray?

Here, in *Tom'chei T'mimim*, for the first time, he realized that *Shabbos* holds special significance. Now he understood that, even within the realm of of spirituality, *Shabbos* is its very highest pinnacle; even within general service of *Hashem*, the special service on *Shabbos* is on an infinitely greater level. *Shabbos* is the "Holy of Holies" for inner spiritual service of *Hashem*, when everything focuses around prayer, which the *Zohar* calls the "backbone" of service of *Hashem* – the *Shabbos* prayers.

The *ma'amar* of *Chassidus* that his new friend now studied with Elimelech discusses the two types of Divine light with which *Hashem* enlivens and sustains the universe: the immanent light of *m'malei kol almin* which fills all the worlds with a life-force that sustains every being according to its defining character, and the transcendent light of *soveiv kol almin*, which encompasses all creation equally without any difference between various beings. It explained the fundamental difference between these two emanations, which is a cornerstone by which *Chassidus* explains countless concepts, such as the life-forces enlivening the soul and body, miracles and nature, the present era and the era of the future, creation of existence from nothingness, essential life, and so on.

To clarify the concept, the *ma'amar* uses an analogy of the powers of the soul. With great elaboration, it explains the difference between the power of will and the other soul powers, such as intellect, sight, hearing, touch, etc. The latter powers are termed "internal" powers because they are enclothed within the body's limbs, fully corresponding to the character of each limb. Thus, the power of sight differs from the power of hearing, and each differs greatly from the power of intellect. That is because each power changes according to the part of the body in which it is enclothed. In contrast, the power of will, which functions equally through all parts of the body, is called an encompassing power because it is not enclothed within any one limb and is never limited to the level of any of them but affects them all equally.

In clear and simple terms, the *ma'amar* explains the advantages and disadvantages of each of these powers. The advantage of a power functioning through a particular limb is that its influence is deeper and fundamental. Since it becomes united with the limb and works directly with it, that limb is fully directed by it in an inner, authentic manner. On the other hand, this inner power has the drawback that it is limited. It cannot compare at all to the soul's essential powers, because this power has to be limited to the nature of the limb to which it belongs. From this perspective, the power of will has a tremendous advantage, for it is unlimited and unrestricted. Yet this encompassing power of will has its own drawback: Because it is not enclothed in the body, its influence is superficial to it, exerting control over the body by force, without effecting any fundamental, lasting change.

After explaining in detail the difference between the soul's internal and encompassing powers, the *ma'amar* moved on to explain the analog, based on the verse "From my flesh I see G-d." The "internal radiances" and "encompassing radiances," the Divine radiances that bring into existence and enliven the universe, are termed, respectively, the "light that fills all worlds" (*m'malei kol almin*) and the "light that encompasses all worlds" (*sovev kol almin*). After the great elaboration of the analogy's details, it became easier to understand the analog, as well as its implications.

This was the first time Elimelech had studied such a deep, intellectual *ma'amar* of *Chassidus*. He found it fascinating. The feeling enveloping him was so uplifting, pure and holy. He felt he had entered a new world of holy and pure concepts, where everything had a new meaning.

The two-hour study session seemed to pass like just a few moments, and the sight of hundreds of students immersed in exalted concepts of *Chassidus*, studying with enthusiasm and shining faces, made a powerful impression, giving him a feeling he had never experienced.

The following *Kabbalas Shabbos* prayers, too, differed utterly from anything he had ever experienced. He found himself praying effortlessly with enthusiasm and passion, arising as a natural result of feelings arising in his heart from studying the *ma'amar* of *Chassidus*.

The inspiring prayers were followed by the *Shabbos* meal, which itself became an inspiring experience. All the students joined in singing the beautiful and profound Chassidic melodies, forming an impressive "choir" that transformed the seemingly ordinary activity of imbibing food into a spiritual experience.

Before he went to sleep for the night, Elimelech mentally summarized everything he had seen, heard, and experienced in his few hours within *Tom'chei T'mimim*. No, all the lavish praises he had heard about the yeshiva were not at all exaggerated. So far there had not been even a single moment of disappointment. Now he was really looking forward to what tomorrow would bring.

Next morning he noticed how careful all students were to wash *negel vasser* next their beds. Soon they ran to immerse themselves in the *mikva*. Before reciting the morning blessings, they washed their hands again as for *negel vasser*, but this time holding the quart-jug with a towel, and then recited the *Sh'ma* before the prescribed time.

Soon they were all sitting together again in pairs in front of their books of *Chassidus*, as the study hall quickly filled with the mighty roar of their voices reading and discussing the texts studied. Elimelech's new friend explained to him that the *Shabbos* prayers are the main way we serve *Hashem* on *Shabbos*, and all preparations before them are meant to ensure deeper inspiration in prayer.

Elimelech asked to review the *maamar* they had studied the night before. This time he noticed many details he had missed the first time. The correspondence between the analogy and its analog now became sharper and the concept in general became much clearer.

After the study session, Eliemelech deliberated his options.

Last night, he had felt the taste of authentic prayer. Now again, with his heart warmed by study of *Chassidus*, he felt a powerful desire to pray devoutly and enthusiastically. On the other hand, his main reason for coming to visit the yeshiva was to observe how the *T'mimim* prayed. Should he interrupt his prayers to focus on watching how they pray?

In the end, he decided his own prayers were more important and it would not be right to interrupt his own focus on his prayers, even for the sake of observing the *T'mimim*. The prayers of the *minyan* proceeded slowly at a patient pace, and he found himself completely absorbed in the holy words he was saying, not noticing his surroundings at all.

The prayers concluded. Gradually, many students left for the dining hall to eat their *Shabbos* meal. Elimelech remained in the study hall a little longer, asking his new friend some questions and listening to his replies.

A few minutes later, Elimelech noticed something interesting. Scattered across the large hall, dozens of students were still sitting or standing alone. They were not talking to each other, nor studying Torah. Each had a deeply serious look on his face. A few sat with heads resting on their arms, eyes closed, but clearly they were not sleeping. Others were gently swaying, stopping occasionally for a moment, then continuing their soft motion. Their lips moved, but with little audible sound. Most gazed intently into their *siddurim*, while others prayed with closed eyes.

Elimelech froze. These must be the *"ovdim"* of *Tom'chei T'mimim*, about whom he had heard so much. He asked his new friend whether these *ovdim* had prayed so long last night, too. He felt bad for having missed it. This was why he had come here!

He forgot any hunger. For a long time, he sat entranced, watching those *ovdim* pray. He had never seen such prayer in his life. Yes, he had seen prayers full of enthusiasm, usually accompanied by grand body movements and loud cries, often intended to impress others. But never had he seen such quiet, powerful prayer, with such intense concentration, without conspicuousness or external show. To witness this alone, it was worth coming, he told himself.

Near him stood a student, about his own age. On the surface one could not detect anything special. His face was not flushed, his movements were not excited, his voice could hardly be heard. He barely moved at all. Yet Elimelech could not take his eyes off him. It took him a while to realize what was so special about this *oved*'s prayer. The student was simply standing and speaking to *Hashem*, the King of all Kings. It was clear that he truly felt himself to be standing before *Hashem* and praying to Him.

Elimelech decided to try and hear the *oved*'s voice as he prayed. Feigning to be looking for some book, he quietly approached where the *oved* was standing, and placed himself behind him with his back to him, pretending to read the book he picked up. The *oved* was up to the blessings before *Sh'ma*. Elimelech heard him whisper with deep feeling, *Ein aroch L'cho Hashem Elokeinu* – "There is none comparable to You, G-d, our Master..." He paused for a moment before continuing, *bo'olom hazeh* – "in this world." A short pause again and then Elimelech heard his voice, "*v'ein zulos'cho Malkeinu, l'chayei ho'olom habo* – "And there is none beside You, our King, in the life of the world of the future." The *oved* sang the words so sweetly, in a way that penetrated Elimelech's heart to its very core. Elimelech stood there, his whole being riveted on the *oved* praying behind him with all his soul.

The *oved* finished the paragraph, and started humming to himself a profoundly inspiring Chabad melody. Elimelech sensed that the *oved* was "living" the melody, transforming it into a part of his prayer. It was as if every one of the melody's movements and individual notes spoke, becoming one with his prayers. Elimelech felt a powerful sense of envy in his heart; he would give anything to pray this way, with all his heart and soul.

It was almost painful to have to tear himself away in order to observe other *ovdim* praying. He noticed the elderly *Mashpia*, deep in prayer. He was still in the middle of *P'sukei d'Zimra*, the first part of the *Shacharis* prayer. As Elimelech passed by, he heard him start singing the words to the Chabad melody so characteristic of Chabad prayer, which was used by the Rebbes of Chabad and their great Chassidim. Every word shook Elimelech's very soul to its core – speaking, pleading, and moving him deeply. He was overwhelmed.

It was perhaps an hour and a half after the *minyan* had finished before Elimelech finally tore himself away to go to eat. The students who had gone to eat immediately had already left, and now many who had prayed longer than everyone else had arrived in the dining hall. It was such a pleasure to be in their company. After their long immersion in devout prayer, their faces shone with an exalted light and their entire manner seemed permeated with nobility and purity. Their conversation was full of *yiras Shamayim* and Chassidic spirit. As they related Chassidic stories and told each other words of Torah and *Chassidus* from the Rebbes and that they had heard from senior Chassidim, their meal became a mini-*farbrengen*. Elimelech was enthralled.

The special atmosphere in the dining hall continued for long, as more and more of the *ovdim* who had prayed at length joined them. Some left when they finished eating, while others came to replace them. Compared to these students, Elimelech felt lowly and unrefined. Their random words and expressions showed him just how coarse were his conceptions, how far his conception of spirituality was from authentic spirituality. This was despite his having studied *Chassidus* for some time, and despite having started to pray according to the Chabad approach and his efforts to adjust his perspective to that of *Chassidus*. The students here seemed to be living on a different planet.

A single thought filled his mind throughout: This is where the truth can be found; here is the source of truth. Whoever is searching for truth, repulsed by whatever he senses to be false, this is his place. Yes, he will need to toil hard, to be ready to submit to challenge, to forgo physical pleasure. But if he persists, this is where he will find the truth!

That *Shabbos* the *Mashpia* did not lead a *farbrengen* for the students, which disappointed Elimelech no end. But the special time of *Raava d'ravin*, from after *Mincha* until the end of *Shabbos*, seemed to compensate. All students sat close together, singing soul-stirring Chabad melodies one after another, repeating each one several times, slowly and with deep feeling. The transition from one melody to the next seemed to come naturally, as if all were links in an unfolding chain of longing and yearning for *Hashem*, for truth, and for revelation of the soul.

Night fell and darkness enveloped the yeshiva, but the students continued to sing those time-honored Chabad melodies, immersed in a world of light and inspiration. After a number of these inspiring melodies, one of the students repeated by heart a *ma'amar* of *Chassidus*, of which Elimelech was pleased to discover that he understood most of it.

After *Shabbos*, Elimelech watched the *T'mimim* studying *Gemara* in pairs with the same passion as during their *Chassidus* study sessions on *Shabbos*. Towards the end of the session, one of the students stood up to share a *pilpul*, a lecture of his Talmudic insights based on his own research, with all the other students. Elimelech was very impressed by the straightforward explanations and logical thought process the student displayed. Other students prodded him with highly relevant questions, and the speaker responded brilliantly. Later, Elimelech found out that the lecturer was one of the outstanding students selected to be the "seven branches of the *menora*," to illuminate and inspire the entire yeshiva (a move originally based on the Rebbe's suggestion).

On his return from *Shabbos* in *Tom'chei T'mimim*, Elimelech finally had some conception of what he had been missing and of the direction to which he ought to aspire.

CHAPTER TWENTY
ON THE WAY TO THE GOAL

Bentzion was not at all aware of what Elimelech had been experiencing in recent weeks. For various reasons, Elimelech had chosen not to share with him about his entrance to the world of Chassidic prayer and his visit to *Tom'chei T'mimim*. They continued to meet twice a week to study *Tanya*.

Yet Bentzion did discern that Elimelech was now placing ever more emphasis on *avoda*, on matters relating to Divine service. He was now speaking more often about deep *avoda* as being the entire purpose of *Chassidus*, and that study of *Chassidus* is but a means to an end, a tool to achieve success in inner Divine service.

Bentzion could not ignore this change, for it was diametrically opposed to his own approach. His primary motivation for studying *Chassidus* was his tremendous yearning to understand everything on a deeper level, to penetrate the secrets of the soul, to uncover the fundamentals of creation, to grasp the inner meaning of the *mitzvos* and the soul accomplishment of Torah study. That was what he sought in studying *Chassidus*. And as soon as he realized he was finding the answers he sought, he could not cover ground quickly enough. His desire to study, to cover another chapter, to understand another concept, only grew. From his point of view, all Elimelech's repeated emphasis on *avoda*, Divine service, was a distraction from the main point, and the more Elimelech dwelled on it, the more the discrepancy disturbed him.

At a certain point, he realized that Elimelech was doing it purposefully, intentionally diverting the focus of their study from emphasis on the intellectual aspects of *Chassidus* to a more practical approach, to the world of *avoda*. Often Elimelech would quote the saying of our Sages, "No one is as wise as someone with experience," explaining that without the "experience" of *Chassidus*, the inner *avoda* demanded by *Chassidus*, it is impossible to become "wise," to understand the intellectual aspects of *Chassidus*. Bentzion started to realize more and more that Elimelech was directing these comments to him personally.

When they started studying Chapter 3 of *Tanya*, Bentzion's suspicions were confirmed. As they studied about the structure of the intellectual and emotional powers of the soul, Bentzion swallowed every word of Elimelech's explanations of the essence of the power of *chachma* (wisdom), and about the length, breadth and depth of comprehension that *bina* (understanding) contributes to the initial flash of *chachma*. He asked so many questions, and Elimelech tried to answer them as best he could.

As they continued to study the chapter, which then discusses the process by which the emotions of love and awe are aroused as a result of the intellectual powers of *chachma* and *bina*, Elimelech realized that Bentzion was impatiently waiting for the end of the chapter where it explains the meaning of *daas* (awareness).

But Elimelech was in no rush. He enjoyed studying about how the intellectual powers arouse the heart to love and feel awe for *Hashem*. When he saw that Bentzion was not particularly interested in that, he decided it was time to talk to him about it.

"What do you think is unique about Chabad in comparison to other approaches of *Chassidus*?" he suddenly asked Bentzion.

"What does that have to do with this subject?" asked Bentzion, buying time to consider the reason for this unexpected question.

"I'll soon tell you how my question is connected to this subject," Elimelech replied, "but first answer my question."

"That's simple," Bentzion answered. "The uniqueness of Chabad *Chassidus* is as its name implies – its emphasis on *chachma*, *bina* and *daas*, on intellect. It requires one to understand everything, and not to suffice with faith alone, despite its importance, but to reach a fundamental understanding of all subjects."

"And what's the purpose of all that understanding?" Elimelech continued to prod.

"How should I know?" Bentzion wondered. "Study and understanding are ends in themselves. It's even a *mitzva*, as it states (*Divrei HaYamim*-Chronicles I, 28:9) 'Know the G-d of your father.' That's what the RaMBaM writes at the beginning of his great code of *Halacha*: 'It is the foundation of all foundations and the pillar of all wisdoms to know...' So knowledge of *Hashem* is important, even a *mitzva*."

"That's all true," Elimelech agreed. "It's important and it's a *mitzva*. But there's another goal, a very basic one. When we study *halachos* in the *Shulchan Aruch*, we're fulfilling the *mitzva* of Torah study, but obviously that *halacha* study is first and foremost for one basic purpose: to guide us on how to fulfill *Hashem*'s Will. The practical outcome is the main point, because, as our Sages say, 'Action is the main point.' The same applies to study of *Chassidus*, which is great in its own right, but also has a very practical primary goal. Have you never heard about this?"

"You must mean that *Chassidus* study should arouse one to serve *Hashem* enthusiastically," Bentzion answered, "to help him overcome his negative traits, to arouse within him a desire to study the Torah and fulfill the *mitzvos*."

"Correct," Elimelech agreed, "but how does this demonstrate Chabad's uniqueness over other paths of *Chassidus*?"

Bentzion had no answer. He really had no idea what Elimelech was driving at. Why had he stopped in the middle of their study of an interesting topic?

"That's the problem," Elimelech started explaining. "Many delve into *Chassidus* but forget its main point, that this profound Torah subject has a clearly defined purpose. *Chassidus* in general seeks to arouse the Jew's soul to become connected with *Hashem* through studying His Torah and fulfilling His commandments. It seeks to infuse him with love and awe of *Hashem*, with joy and trust in Him. This always has been and still remains the basic purpose of *Chassidus*.

"So how is this done? How does a *Chassid* succeed in rising above the mundane world and his material conceptions to reach such an exalted level of serving *Hashem*?

"This is why *Chassidus* includes the concept of a Rebbe, a *tzaddik*. The Rebbe is a holy person on a highly exalted level, who has been endowed with a lofty soul and special powers. He has succeeded in reaching the highest levels of love and awe of

Hashem. Empowered by all this, the Rebbe can also raise up any *Chassid* connected with him, who follows his directives, who spends time close to him. This must lead to the *Chassid* becoming uplifted, too. Before Chabad, many Chassidic leaders would read the verse in Chabakuk (2:4), *Tzaddik be'emunoso yichyeh* – 'A *tzaddik* lives by his faith' – with a slight change of vowels: 'Do not read *yichyeh* [he lives] but *yechayeh* [he enlivens],' in other words, he revitalizes others connected with him with spiritual vitality. Just his great faith, and his love and awe of *Hashem*, his spiritual greatness alone, are sufficient to inject spiritual vitality into everyone connected to him, without their having to invest effort of their own.

"But then came the Alter Rebbe, author of the *Tanya*, and taught that we should not rely only on the Rebbe. The *Chassid*'s motivation should never come from an external source. Otherwise, the *Chassid* will remain essentially as he always was; he has not refined or elevated himself properly to full perfection, because he was never required to achieve anything on his own steam, but always relied only on his Rebbe. That's why the Alter Rebbe directed that we approach it differently: The main motivation must come from within oneself, working on oneself to refine one's personal traits, to rid oneself of materiality, to arouse within oneself love and awe of *Hashem*.

"The Rebbe's role is to help the Chassid even further, to guide him and give him the tools, by beaming upon the *Chassid* his holy powers, to give the *Chassid* blessings that help him advance in his *avodas Hashem*. But the connection with the Rebbe should never replace or come at the expense of the Chassid's personal service of *Hashem*.

"So what empowers the *Chassid* to rise higher and to arouse his love and awe of *Hashem*? Surely that's expected of every Jew, even an ordinary Jew not on a high level, who's not endowed with a lofty soul. How can he uplift himself?

"In actual practice, he does this with Chabad *Chassidus*. The Alter Rebbe taught that everyone has an inner impetus enabling us to uplift ourselves to reach the desired goal. It's the intellect. Everyone has a brain in his head, which he can put to good use. It doesn't depend on anything but one's own choice; the use of one's intellect depends only on one's will. Through the intellect, one can achieve love and awe of *Hashem* and refinement of one's character."

Bentzion had listened to Elimelech's long explanation without response. But now he felt compelled to question this last point. "What do you mean by that? The intellect can understand and know, but how does it bring one to experience feelings of love and awe?"

Elimelech smiled. "That's exactly what we're studying about here in Chapter 3. But you're so impatient that you're rushing to get to the end of the chapter to find out about *daas*...

"Actually, the intellect isn't just the instrument for understanding and knowing. It's also a means for controlling the emotions. It has the power to arouse desirable emotions and to weaken or even cancel undesirable emotions. It's almost as if the intellect can do anything, on condition, of course, that we know how to use it.

"Now pay attention to what the Alter Rebbe says here:

"'The intellect in the rational soul, when it reflects on and delves very deeply into the greatness of G-d, how He fills all worlds and encompasses all worlds, and how, before Him, everything is considered as nothing, there is born and aroused in his mind and thought a feeling of awe for the Divine greatness, to be overawed and humbled by G-d's exalted greatness, which is endless and unlimited, and of dread of G-d in one's heart.'

"What do we learn from here? That the emotions aroused in one's heart depend upon what he thinks and on what he reflects. It's not easy, of course, to generate emotions of love and awe. Notice how the Alter Rebbe emphasizes: '...When it reflects on and delves very deeply.' But when one does indeed meditate and forces himself to think very deeply for a long while and with concentration, then he does succeed in arousing within himself the feelings commensurate with his meditation. In the case discussed here, when one meditates on *Hashem*'s greatness, on how He fills all worlds and encompasses all worlds and is the sole existence of all Creation, because 'Before Him everything is considered as nothing,' then such a meditation will instill within him a recognition of *Hashem*'s immense greatness, so that awe of Him becomes aroused in one's heart.

"But as soon as one feels awe, he'll perceive another aspect to his meditation. When he comes to recognize *Hashem*'s immense greatness, and how He gives life and existence to all Creation, then, following the awe, his heart becomes aroused also with love for *Hashem*:

"'Next, his heart will become enthused with an intense love, like burning coals, with a passion, desire and longing, and a yearning soul, for the greatness of the Infinite One, blessed be He. This is the soul's self-consuming passion, as is stated [*Tehilim*-Psalms 84:3], as 'My soul longs, and even becomes consumed...,' and 'My soul thirsts for G-d...' [ibid. 42:2], and 'My soul thirsts for You...' [ibid. 63:2]."

"From all this we learn that the intellect has the power to change one's essential nature. The intellect thinks and reflects, resulting in the heart becoming aroused, so that appropriate feelings are aroused and negative emotions vanish. So everything depends on the intellect.

"But the intellect has to have what to think about. We're referring to the need to generate feelings of love and awe of *Hashem*, and eagerness to fulfill the *mitzvos* and study the Torah, by means of concepts abstract and refined. Natural human intellect, on its own, has no grasp of these concepts and is unable to reflect on them. That's why the Alter Rebbe revealed Chabad *Chassidus*, which enables us to fulfill his special approach. As I explained, this approach holds that one needs to work with his own abilities, among which the intellect is the main driving force. That's why it's so important to give the intellect subjects on which to reflect on the Divine. Those subjects are the content of Chabad *Chassidus*, in which the most exalted Divine concepts are expressed in terms accessible to understanding and comprehension, so that even the mind of an ordinary person, like mine or yours, is able to grasp them. And since we understand, we have what to think about and it's possible to accomplish the primary goal.

"So let's summarize: Study of *Chassidus* is not an end in itself, but an essential ingredient in the Chabad path of serving

Hashem. Studying *Chassidus* for the sake of study alone, merely in order to know and understand the concepts, while forgetting about the *avoda* implicit in the words of *Chassidus*, means emphasizing what's secondary and neglecting what's most important."

Throughout Elimelech's long explanation, Bentzion was listening attentively, trying to understand what he was driving at. He guessed that his friend was trying to convey a specific message, but remained unsure exactly what that message was. Suddenly, what Elimelech meant hit him; he grasped what he was implying about his approach to *Chassidus* until then.

Elimelech noticed how Bentzion had suddenly frozen. Appreciating what must be going through his mind, the moment seemed ripe to strike while the iron was hot. He decided to express his feelings without restraint.

"Bentzion!" Elimelech aroused him from his trance. "Until now, you've been studying *Chassidus* as a replacement for philosophy. After you became convinced that studying intellectual philosophy is harmful, you decided to exchange it for *Chassidus*. But *Chassidus* isn't philosophy. It isn't pure intellectualism, nor is it abstract ideas aimed at explaining everything with which to answer your intellectual curiosity. *Chassidus* is a path in serving *Hashem*. It's to assist a Jew in serving *Hashem*. That's its goal and purpose. It's impossible to take only the intellectual aspect of *Chassidus*. You have to do something with it, to work with it. Your whole approach to *Chassidus* needs to change!"

His words reached directly to their goal. Bentzion sat with his head lowered, listening to every word. Elimelech's message was as clear as day. For long the two sat silently, deep in thought. Bentzion began to sense how his attitude toward *Chassidus* was changing. Penetrating his mind was the realization that *Chassidus* is not just attractive but also obligates, that it is not enough to study it as theoretical ideas but that one needs to immerse himself in its practical side, too. Now he started to become fascinated with the *avoda*, too, of *Chassidus*. From the several of its concepts that he already understood properly, he realized how far he still was from the truth. The concept of *avoda* began to speak to his heart.

CHAPTER TWENTY-ONE

THE INNER STRUGGLE

Both Elimelech and Bentzion were excited by the new revelations to which they had been exposed in the world of *Chassidus*. Meanwhile, however, Aharon was experiencing a difficult mini-crisis. His study-partner Bentzion had given him no inkling of his introduction to *Chassidus*, so he assumed Aharon was unaware of it. But Aharon had realized it. He once noticed a pocket-sized *Tanya* peeking out his friend's jacket pocket. He was surprised at how careful Bentzion was suddenly becoming, when praying and reciting blessings, to wear two head coverings, as per Chabad custom, and how he had started to wear his *talis koton* over his pajamas when he went to sleep. He could not help but notice many other small changes gradually becoming evident in his companion's conduct.

Aharon always had a special talent to infer the bigger picture from small, seemingly isolated details. Not much more was needed for him to realize that Bentzion was gradually accepting the Chassidic way of life in full. When Bentzion started waking up early to leave their room quietly, trying to hide a towel under his jacket, Aharon realized he was on his way to the *mikva*. Every now and then, Bentzion took on new customs typical of Chassidim, and Aharon noticed it.

Externally, nothing changed. The two continued their study-partnership and remained good friends. They discussed every other topic that came up. But both sensed a secret wall rising between them. Sensing that Aharon's negative reaction to his

234

study of philosophy would recur if he heard about his study of *Chassidus*, Bentzion decided not to share his experiences with him. Aharon, on the other hand, did not want to reveal what he realized, so he continued to pretend to see and hear nothing. But the silence started to bother him more and more.

For long he forced himself to ignore the issue and minimize its importance. Repeatedly he told himself it had nothing to do with him. All that was required of him was to sit and study, knowing of nothing besides Torah study. But even without Bentzion breathing a word about it, the many changes in him were leaving their mark. Gradually Aharon sensed how his stubborn opposition was melting away, with envy taking its place. He saw Bentzion blossoming, progressing and advancing. In Bentzion's speech, small changes hinted at new, more exalted concepts and a more wholesome perspective that he was incorporating into his view of life and of man's mission in the world. Seeing and hearing all this, Aharon felt more and more left behind, indeed shallow, in comparison with his friend's new world full of richness and depth.

His own shallowness began to depress him. Before mentioning it once in a conversation with Elimelech, he had never paid attention to it and certainly it never occurred to him to label it as shallowness. At first glance, what could be more meaningful than living as a Torah scholar, who had nothing more in life than the Talmudic discussions of Abbaye and Rova? Most of his waking hours were occupied with Torah study, clarifying difficult Talmudic subjects, ascribing importance to nothing beyond the world of Torah. But after having already received, from his long discussions with Elimelech, the background to understand what he now saw in Bentzion, his only way to define what he felt was to realize it was shallowness. Clearly Bentzion knew exactly why he was studying Torah, feeling its holiness and exalted greatness. He seemed to have a continuous flame burning within him by the light of which he studied Torah, prayed, and fulfilled *mitzvos*. Within Aharon, on the other hand, no such spiritual fire burned. Deep within him, he felt cold, dry and lifeless.

He could have gone on living that way all his life. Had he never seen and realized that there could be another way, it might never have disturbed him much. Now, however, he could not delude himself: Bentzion's and Elimelech's shining faces never left his mind, teasing and mocking him, poking fun at his immature conceptions and struggles and at the stagnation within him.

If only he had some way to release all his pent-up emotion by having someone with whom to share and discuss it, to work it out together, then it would be easier. But now he had no one. His relationship with Elimelech had been disrupted, and a wall of silence now stood between him and Bentzion. Sometimes it felt as though his friend's silence almost made him go out of his mind, so desperately did he feel the need to discuss the issue right away!

But Bentzion did not talk. It was almost insulting that while Bentzion was advancing and growing, Aharon felt left behind. While they could study a page of *Gemara* together, apparently Bentzion could not talk to him about serving *Hashem* and spirituality. For that he had Elimelech.

When Bentzion had studied philosophy, and Aharon had

rebuked and guided him and shown him the true path, it had boosted Aharon to feel stronger and on a higher spiritual level. Now, however, slowly but surely, their roles had been transposed. Aharon sensed that Bentzion was growing and accomplishing much more than he, while he remained far down below, from where he looked up longingly at his friend's exalted new world. Bentzion now seemed to surpass him in everything, studying with greater diligence and enthusiasm, praying more intensely, fulfilling *mitzvos* with much more *hiddur*, paying attention to details to which Aharon had never attached significance. There seemed to be some internal "motor" propelling Bentzion forward, while Aharon, who now tried to imitate him, felt like a young child playing catch up with a racing car roaring at high speed.

***

One Thursday evening, as the two studied together, Aharon felt a heavy fatigue overcome him. However he tried to prevent it failed. He had no choice but to ask Bentzion to excuse him and wake him in an hour, while he rested his head on his arms and fell asleep.

He awoke with a start. His tiredness seemed to evaporate as his senses focused on a conversation he heard from across the room, and he strained not to miss a single word. Bentzion was talking quietly to another student, explaining the Chassidic concept of inward *avoda*. Aharon understood that the other student had apparently started to show interest in *Chassidus*.

Avoda p'nimis – "inward service" of *Hashem* – Bentzion was telling him, includes two main aspects. The first is to rid oneself of coarseness and materiality. The second is to infuse the body and soul with the light of Torah and holiness.

"Both are necessary," Bentzion emphasized. "Without removing the coarseness and materiality, it's like pouring fine wine into a dirty cup. In fact it's even worse. On the physical level, we can actually pour fine wine into a filthy cup, but on the spiritual level, not only do coarseness and materiality coarsen and spoil spirituality, but they don't allow it to be absorbed at all. That's why it's essential first to refine our body and animal soul. Of course, refinement on its own is not enough, because although you'll have a proper vessel, it'll be devoid of light and holiness. So we need the second step, too, to infuse oneself with light and spirituality.

"How do we prepare our body and animal soul to become fitting receptacles?" Bentzion continued. "We do it by breaking our desires." Aharon's ears were not missing a word.

"Chassidim have a saying, 'What is forbidden is certainly forbidden, and what is permitted is unnecessary!' Even what the Torah permits us to eat and do, when we do it out of natural desire and not for the sake of Heaven, it can harm the soul. That's why we have the concept called *iskafiya* – self-discipline – which means subduing the animal soul and reining it in through denying not only what's forbidden but even what's permitted. Anything not essential for maintaining the body is superfluous and is therefore harmful. Every individual can find his own point of *iskafiya*. Sometimes it means not finishing everything on our plate and leaving something. Or *iskafiya* can be expressed the opposite way, by eating a food we dislike. Both these approaches subdue our animal soul. But completely unnecessary foods like candy and other pleasure foods are absolutely out of the question. Whoever wants to serve *Hashem* needs to keep away from all that to the extreme."

The other student asked, "But didn't I once hear that *Chassidus* doesn't encourage fasting and self-mortification?"

"True," replied Bentzion, "*Chassidus* doesn't approve of breaking the body by fasting and denying its needs. We don't need to break the body. On the contrary, we need to maintain our health and make sure not to harm the body. The Mezeritcher *Maggid*, who was the Baal Shem Tov's successor and the *Baal HaTanya*'s Rebbe, used to say, 'A small hole in the body is a big hole in the soul.' But that doesn't mean we should indulge everything that our body desires without a second thought. Breaking the body is negative; refining it and ennobling it is essential. And we accomplish that goal through *iskafiya*.

"Your mention of fasting reminds me of an interesting story:

"A *Chassid* once complained to the Rebbe MaHaRaSh (Rabbi Shmuel of Lubavitch, the fourth leader of Chabad, 1834-1882) that he was lacking truth in his heart. 'I view everything through a veil of cunning, crookedness and trickery,' the *Chassid* bemoaned his spiritual state, begging the Rebbe for a blessing to view everything with a pure and honest heart.

"The Rebbe MaHaRaSh's prescription was that he should fast 600 fasts!

"The *Chassid* was shocked, wondering how he could possibly fulfill the Rebbe's directive.

"The Rebbe explained what he meant: 'Do you think fasting

means to abstain from eating from sunrise to sunset? Is that a fast? That's just losing weight. A fast means spiritual effort. It's important that you spend fifteen minutes every day thinking about your spiritual situation. I don't mean by studying *Chassidus*, but simply thinking for fifteen minutes a day about your situation.'

"The Chassid fulfilled this directive and devoted a quarter hour daily just to thinking about himself. The son of the Rebbe MaHaRaSh, the Rebbe RaShaB, who told this story, added that, after two years, that same *Chassid* had utterly transformed his character; those fifteen minutes of self-reflection changed his entire being."

Aharon had been breathing in every word. He now started taking the message to heart. He recalled how, just a few months ago, Bentzion had experienced doubts of faith and was falling lower and lower spiritually, with a cold insensitivity consuming his very soul. Yet now he had changed from one extreme to the other. He was now full of pure *yiras Shamayim*, permeated with the warmth of Torah and holiness, serving *Hashem* and advancing daily in Torah study and *mitzvos* observance. There was no denying that *Chassidus* had accomplished this. Everything is guided from Above, and what had happened to Bentzion was clearly a "descent for the purpose of ascent." He had fallen into intellectual philosophy and arisen from it by way of *Chassidus*.

On the other hand, Aharon thought to himself, although he had never fallen, yet neither had he improved at all. His heart felt void, dry and lifeless. The Torah he studied might fill his brain, but his heart and soul remained parched like a desert. To be honest, he had no idea how to pray, nor really how to relate to anything spiritual.

His eyes started to fill with tears. Never had he experienced such heartfelt distress. Perhaps he, too, should follow that directive of self-reflection for fifteen minutes a day? But as soon as it occurred to him, he dismissed it out of hand. To do that would be false. If the path of *Chassidus* is true, he decided, he ought to enter into it completely, with all his heart and soul. There was no point in playing games by picking and choosing. A hot tear slid down his cheek and fell on his clothes. He was thankful that his head was hidden in his arms, so that no one would notice. His tears provided a measure of relief. His attention wandered back to Bentzion's conversation.

Bentzion was now explaining to that other student the difference between the approaches of *Chassidus* and *mussar* regarding refinement of one's character traits.

"The approach of *mussar*," he explained, "strives to change one's negative traits to positive ones – arrogance into humility, anger and annoyance into kindness and generosity, and so on. *Chassidus* calls that 'changing the natural traits.' The initial difference between the two approaches is in the means of influencing the character traits: Chassidus advocates that a little light repels much darkness, whereas *mussar* teaches one to deal with negative traits directly. Besides that, however, *Chassidus* teaches that there's another fundamental task – changing the very nature of one's character traits. That means that even positive traits need to be worked on so that their very nature becomes changed."

"What do you mean by that?" asked the other student.

"I'll tell you another story," Bentzion said, "which will give you the answer to your question. There once came to the Alter Rebbe a Torah scholar renowned throughout the region for his positive character traits; he was goodhearted, generous and did many kind and charitable deeds.

"The Rebbe asked him, 'What's the difference, from the perspective of character traits, between a human being and an animal? If the difference is that a human being has good character traits, surely there are animals, too, with very positive traits. So where, then, is a human being's superiority over an animal? The answer is that, in an animal, its traits are natural, which is how it was created. On the other hand, a human being's purpose is to make his character traits depend on his intellect, so they not be natural but that the intellect should direct and guide them.'

"When that Torah scholar of wonderful character heard this, he did a rapid self-assessment on the spot and came to the conclusion that, throughout his life, his positive traits had never developed beyond the level of an animal! Realizing this, he fainted and fell to the floor."

"But what does that mean, practically speaking?" the student continued to question.

"It means," Bentzion replied, "that one is expected to control his heart with his mind, to reach a point where not only are his character traits positive and pure, but that they are completely dependent on his intellect; not free and independent but totally controlled by the mind.

"That's the reason why it was specifically the *akeida*, Avrohom's binding of Yitzchok on the altar, that prompted *Hashem* to tell him, 'Now I know that you fear G-d.' At first that seems strange: After Avrohom had already withstood *Hashem*'s first nine difficult tests, didn't *Hashem* know by then that Avrohom feared Him? The answer is that, until that time, his service of *Hashem* had possibly been purely natural, resulting from his basic good nature and essential soul character that made him feel intense love of *Hashem* and for his fellow human beings, which was how he had passed all the other tests. Yet now, when faced with the test of the *akeida*, Avrohom, despite his outstandingly good and kind nature, was showing how, to fulfill *Hashem*'s will, he was prepared to go against every fiber of his nature. He would even do something so cruel, to sacrifice his only son, solely because *Hashem* had commanded him. It was that which proved that Avrohom was truly G-d fearing."

When Bentzion awoke him from his feigned sleep, Aharon was gripped by an overpowering inner conflict. He felt that the moment of truth was approaching.

CHAPTER TWENTY-TWO
THE FATEFUL NIGHT

Perhaps Bentzion sensed the storm brewing in Aharon's heart. Or perhaps not, but he had decided the time had finally come to talk. Either way, he decided to utilize an opening that might lead his friend into a meaningful conversation: That evening was Aharon's eighteenth birthday.

When Bentzion reminded him of that, Aharon responded impatiently, "Come on, we're not children anymore."

Bentzion immediately explained he was referring to that special date's spiritual significance. At first Aharon was amused, unsure whether his friend was serious or just teasing. Since he had grown to maturity, it had never occurred to him that birthdays were significant.

But Bentzion was not joking. He was totally serious. He told Aharon that, as he understood, a birthday holds great importance in one's life. It could even be considered as one's personal *Rosh Hashana*, when one's *mazal* (spiritual source) is at its strongest. On that date, one is endowed with spiritual powers to fortify oneself, to rise higher, change negative habits and gain momentum for serving *Hashem* through the coming year.

Such words would most likely have had no effect on Aharon had he not been in his present frame of mind. Now, however, he listened intently to what Bentzion told him about a need to spend time alone on this special day and to make a personal spiritual accounting. Bentzion told him how Chassidim and righteous people would go out into the fields or seclude themselves in a room on their birthdays to think about themselves. They would reflect on all that had happened during the past year and previous years, dwelling upon their memories, and making firm resolutions to improve and rectify any deficiencies for the coming year.

Aharon tried to find in his friend's words some implied reference to *Chassidus*. Perhaps, he thought, Bentzion was finally trying to pierce the wall of silence between them, to open a conversation about *Chassidus*. But Bentzion gave no hint of such an intention. He was talking with utter sincerity, with no hidden agenda.

For his part, though, Aharon remained firm in his decision not to be the one to start any conversation on that subject, no matter what.

***

The idea of seclusion in order to think about himself started to intrigue him, especially in his present emotional state. The last few weeks had been unsettling. He could do nothing without his thoughts confusing him and returning him again and again to the topic from which he so desperately wanted to escape. How had he not thought of that idea himself, to spend some time alone and make a fundamental self-assessment of his whole situation? Throughout those days, he had found himself deliberating over these themes again and again. But his thoughts had been so disorganized. Bentzion's advice and his approaching birthday had come together at the right time.

Sitting on the large rock outside the yeshiva building, the ancient olive tree hanging over him from above, images in his memory of recent years passed before his mind's eye. He recalled all his lengthy late-night conversations with Elimelech in their previous yeshiva's library room. The memories were amazingly clear; he experienced anew every feeling and thought passing then through his mind.

But now he had gained what he had been missing before – the perspective and ability to view everything from the distance of time to get a broader point of view. Previously, they had seemed like isolated incidents, connected perhaps but weakly. Now they combined in his mind to create a complete mosaic. Only now could he connect the dots of everything he had seen and heard but had not understood at the time. Previously these details had been caught up in the intensity of the process. Now, however, the picture was sharp and clear. The shining personalities of Elimelech and Bentzion were convincing proof of the correctness of the ideas they had shared back then.

Meditating on his current state only completed the picture even further. His inner dryness simply screamed out. From deep within his soul he felt an intense longing to get out his hang-ups, to be enveloped in the infinite light of holiness, if only once to taste true outpouring of his soul. But he realized that this desire, concealed deep within his soul, was closed in from all sides within the materiality and coarseness of his physical body, into which spiritual light had never penetrated. His soul cried out within him, but the barrier of his body and his limited conceptions was impenetrable.

Later he would realize that this feeling of distress paining him so deeply for lacking a true feeling of holiness actually proved that something had moved within him, breaching the wall entrapping his soul. Without such a sense of brokenness, one can continue living an entire life in equanimity and self-satisfaction, without it ever occurring that perhaps he was missing something. His feeling of missing something, his self-flagellation born of a sense of parched dryness, was actually a faint glimmer of Divine light. But Aharon would understand this only much later. Now he sat in the middle of the large field, enveloped by the darkness of night, while his heart was torn by a storm of doubts.

He had lived for eighteen years, he thought sadly, the best years of his life when one's personality is formed, laying the foundation for his entire life. Whatever had not been accomplished during those years would likely never be achieved. Right now, his sapling was still young, his soul still tender, his body not yet seriously coarsened. If in those years he had not yet reached a significant spiritual level, how would he achieve anything while caring for a family and perforce involved in mundane matters? If now, with no material worries and nothing distracting him from the world of Torah, his soul had not been moved, how could that happen when he would bear the burden of making a living?

He started to castigate himself. He had once heard from Elimelech that when one's heart is blocked, the solution is to denigrate oneself, to crush one's arrogance and ego into pieces. So he began to call himself by every possible lowly name, telling himself he was like an animal that sees nothing but the grass below, never trying to raise its eyes heavenward; so, too, he had no idea how to view anything other than from a material, animal perspective.

Yes, he studied Torah and appreciated its profound logic. But did he sense its holiness and loftiness? When praying, he thought only of his material needs. All his conceptions were limited and materialistic. His heart was blocked like a stone, and only material concerns excited him, whereas spiritual and refined matters left him utterly indifferent. What, then, made him superior to beasts of the field? How did he deserve to approach study of *Hashem*'s Torah, to be designated a Torah scholar? Did he have the slightest true connection with the Torah's holiness, with *Hashem* who has given us the Torah? Under what kind of delusion was he living?

Indeed, Elimelech's advice was working; the barrier blocking Aharon's heart was suddenly shattered. The distress so tightly bottled up within him in recent weeks was finally released as hot tears streamed down his cheeks. He did not bother wiping them away. It was a relief to be so brutally honest with himself, and to feel the hot tears flowing from his eyes. A lone owl screeched as it flew past, piercing the night's stillness like an echo to his shame and remorse.

But he continued relentlessly. Externally he was viewed as an outstanding student, even a prodigy, praised and envied by everyone. He was assured of a bright future. His teachers hinted that he would be a great Torah leader one day. But only he knew the truth of how coarse he was, drawn after physical desires that embarrassed him even to recall. So passed one day and the next; everyone continued praising him, which made him happy. But those praises masked the bitter reality, and falsehood would continue to penetrate and rot him from within. And after all that, he might actually become a *Rosh Yeshiva* and be teaching students. How could he fall so low?

Suddenly Aharon cried out in frustration, "Enough, it's

impossible to continue this game. I need to shake off this thick mask of falsehood!"

***

Aharon felt a hand on his shoulder. Looking up with a start, he spun around and was shocked to see Bentzion standing still behind him, gazing at him fondly. Slowly Aharon recovered from his confused state. He understood that Bentzion had traced his steps and had witnessed what was happening to him. He realized that Bentzion could not be unaware of the inner conflict raging within him. Overcome with embarrassment, he bowed his head silently.

For the first time in his life, on that night of his eighteenth birthday, under the ancient olive tree, Aharon poured out his heart to another person, baring his soul to his friend. Bentzion was not surprised. He had guessed what lay behind his friend's confused behavior. What did surprise him was how clearly Aharon expressed his pain and his soul's subtle feelings.

For a long time they talked. Aharon unloaded everything that had accumulated inside him, while Bentzion listened intently to every word. He did not need to debate him or convince him of anything. The conclusions were clear to both. After Aharon finished, Bentzion started describing to him how deeply *Chassidus* had impressed and changed him. This time Aharon listened to every word and agreed how right he was.

Dawn had already broken when Aharon suddenly confessed, "*Chassidus* does intrigue me, but I'm afraid it will lessen my diligence in Torah study."

"Aharon," Bentzion replied. "Just now you've realized how all your arguments and preconceived notions of *Chassidus* have proven to be mistaken. Didn't you just agree that you don't really know anything about the true nature of *Chassidus*? And now you're back to repeating the same old errors (although I agree it's a common mistake)."

"I don't know what to say," Aharon stammered, "but that's what everyone else says, right?"

"For sure they say it," Bentzion answered emphatically, "together with many other things, too. But the common denominator of everything they say is that it all couldn't be further from the truth. I do understand where that error originated. Whereas other groups emphasize exclusively Torah study, *Chassidus* emphasizes so much else besides: proper prayer, inward *avoda*, study of *Chassidus*, great care in keeping *mitzvos* with *hiddur*, a soul-connection with the Rebbe. So others get the mistaken impression that Chassidim don't study enough Torah. In fact the truth is the absolute opposite, for *Chassidus* gives us an intense desire to study Torah."

"How?" asked Aharon.

"Without *Chassidus*," Bentzion replied, "one is utterly unaware of the Torah's true significance. Yes, one knows that the Torah is very profound and exalted, 'longer than the earth and wider than the ocean.' But he has no conception of its true essence, and is unable to sense its holiness. He studies about an ox goring a cow, for example, or exchanging a cow for a donkey, about simple claims brought to court. He might know that the Torah's depth is infinite, but has no idea what that means. When someone studies *Chassidus*, however, he suddenly starts to realize the Torah's significance, which gives one much greater desire to study it."

"What, for example, have you learned about what the Torah actually is?" Aharon asked.

"I'll try and explain one idea," Bentzion replied, "and you'll see for yourself the kind of depth that *Chassidus* gives to the actual concept of Torah study. The prophets call the Torah *m'shal HaKadmoni*, 'the analogy for the Original Being.' *Chassidus* explains that this is the essence of the Torah – it's an analogy for *Hashem*. What's an analogy? The way the Torah employs the term, an analogy is not an alien medium through which to understand the analog. It's the analog itself, except that the analogy narrows the analog to its lowest level.

"I'll try to explain that. Our Sages say: 'There is no blade of grass below that does not have a *mazal* – a spiritual source – Above that strikes it and tells it to grow.' *Chassidus* explains that every blade of grass, and every creation, has a higher spiritual source from which its unique characteristics are derived and which causes its growth and existence. If an apple tastes sweet, it's because it derives from spiritual aspect of *chessed* – kindness – within its spiritual source Above. There, on the spiritual plane, the concept of sweetness exists, and from there it comes down into this physical world.

"The process that this spiritual sweetness undergoes until it becomes the physical sweetness of an apple has many stages, of which some are here in our physical world. The highest level is the sweet pleasure of a deep intellectual concept. Below that is the sweetness of music. All these are levels of sweetness, but clearly they are more spiritual and abstract than the physical taste of sweetness. But all these levels of sweetness derive from that same spiritual level of sweetness as it exists in its exalted spiritual source.

"Now let's say we want to describe the sweetness of music to a simple person. We would have no choice but to provide an analogy. We could tell him that just as an apple is sweet, so is music sweet, too. He would have to contemplate the sensation of tasting a sweet apple and then try to understand how sweetness can apply to hearing a beautiful melody. The next level is to use the sweetness of music to serve as an analogy for the sweetness of an intellectual concept, which is a higher level of sweetness. There is this framework of analogies and analogs that are actually derived one from another, yet, at their inner core, constitute a single unified concept.

"This explains the Scriptural verse describing King Shlomo as telling '3,000 analogies.' It doesn't mean that he just related three thousand parables. It means that he would try to explain a certain concept and, in order to bring it down to a simpler level of understanding, he had to use three thousand analogies, each of which served as an analogy for the preceding one. Chassidus explains that King Shlomo's perception was at the lowest level of the exalted spiritual world of *Atzilus*, and in order for his intellectual grasp to be appreciated at a lower level, it had to pass through the three lower spiritual worlds of *B'riya*, *Y'tzira*, and *Asiya*. Each of these worlds has one thousand levels, so King Shlomo had to give three thousand analogies until the concept could be brought down and explained at the simplest level...

"That's the meaning of the words in Scripture, 'The analogy of the Original One,' which refers to the Torah. By definition, the Torah is *Hashem*'s essential wisdom, which is exalted beyond any expression. Yet *Hashem* enclothed this Torah and lowered it through an infinite number of levels, where each level is an analogy for the preceding one. The Torah that we have is the material analogy for the real Torah, its 'garment' in our physical world. There's a certain advantage to this, for the Torah was not given to the angels, but specifically to us Jews, who grasp the Torah through its physical 'garments.' In its true essence, however, the Torah is far more exalted than 'an ox which gored a cow' or than 'two who argue over ownership of a cloak'; it's even beyond any spiritual description. Any expression or 'garment' of the Torah is just an analogy, and we are required to try and penetrate to a higher level of understanding, the analog of the analogy, which is itself an analogy for what preceded it.

"This is the true meaning of the Torah's infinite nature: It includes analogies and analogs, one higher than the other, infinitely, which is why the Torah is 'longer than the earth and wider than the ocean.'"

"But we're unable to understand those higher spiritual levels," Aharon observed.

"First of all, that's not true," Bentzion clarified. "Obviously we're unable to understand the Torah as it's studied in *Gan Eden*, but we certainly have the ability to understand its higher levels in this world. But that's not the important point, as much as the perspective on Torah that this explanation gives us. When I first learned this concept, I started to relate to the Torah completely differently, and also felt that I wanted to study it much more than I ever had, so that my intellect would be enveloped by the Torah's exalted holiness."

Quietly the two walked back to the yeshiva building. The glorious sunrise starting to send its radiance between the mountains did not distract their profound thoughts, for what had occurred that night had life-changing significance for them both.

CHAPTER TWENTY-THREE
"HOW FORTUNATE WE ARE, HOW GOOD IS OUR PORTION!"

Intense preparations were underway among Lubavitcher Chassidim. The anticipation increased as the momentous occasion approached. Every *Chassid* connected with the Rebbe and Chabad *Chassidus* looked forward to the date with mounting excitement. All who were able had already arranged their places to stay in the Rebbe's neighborhood to be there on that special day.

As the date approached, the great flow of visitors swelled. The *beis hamidrash* at 770 Eastern Parkway in Crown Heights, Brooklyn, filled with Chassidim from all over the world. Every day masses of new faces appeared, and in every corner Chassidim greeted each other warmly with a heartfelt *sholom aleichem*, eyes shining with joy as they noticed familiar faces they had not seen for years. Many of those now meeting each other had studied together in *Tomchei T'mimim* years before but had since scattered round the world. A warm atmosphere of true brotherly affection filled the *beis hamidrash* and the entire neighborhood.

Every evening, groups of Chassidim held brotherly *farbrengens*. They compared memories, related to each other beautiful stories that had happened to them or to Jews in their community, exchanged responses received from the Rebbe on their queries and discussed their implications. The yeshiva students surrounding them swallowed thirstily their every word, especially when they recalled memories of *Tom'chei T'mimim* and their revered *Mashpi'im* in times past. The impressive personalities of the Chassidim leading and participating in these *farbrengens* seemed clearly to validate the special education these yeshivos had given their students; present students could witness with their own eyes what classic Chassidic education had produced.

The meeting of Aharon, Bentzion, and Elimelech was very emotional. Over ten years ago each had left for a different part of the world to accomplish his unique mission. Their pressing day-to-day concerns of family and vocation had weakened the ties between them, and this momentous occasion was a fitting opportunity for them to reconnect, for which they were overjoyed.

On first entering *Yeshivas Tom'chei T'mimim* in Kfar Chabad, they had studied for several years together before proceeding to the yeshiva at 770, close to the Rebbe. After they married, however, each had gone on his separate way, studying for several years at a *kollel* in a different location. Before long, each had been offered an important position, whether in Torah education or in spreading *Yiddishkeit*.

Bentzion became a *shaliach* of the Rebbe to one of the American states, where he enjoyed immense success. In just a few years he succeeded in establishing a flourishing community, with all the institutions required in a religious Jewish community, from preschool to *yeshiva gedola*. He had become internationally famous as a talented speaker, drawing large crowds to his lectures and holding audiences spellbound by his informative explanations of Torah and *Chassidus*. He had a unique ability to draw his listeners to listen attentively, and his conclusions were so clear and straightforward that his audience would feel them to be the obvious truth. He became one of the most powerful forces worldwide for attracting Jews to reinforce their *Yiddishkeit* and in showing the path for *baalei teshuva*.

Elimelech, of course, had a very different personality. In yeshiva already, he had been regarded as an exemplary *oved*. His whole being expressed *avoda*. He might not have had Bentzion's quick, bright mind, but in every aspect of inward personal *avoda* he was an outstanding model. With iron willpower and self-discipline, he would focus powerfully for hours on concepts of *Chassidus*, and study Torah diligently even when exhausted. Whenever there was some difficult challenge that others tried to avoid, Elimelech would tackle it head on. His fellow students regarded him as a model of one who sets aside his own wishes, who did not function as a self-aware existence; his entire being was defined by his bond with the Rebbe and sense of obligation to fulfill his directives.

It was no surprise, then, when Elimelech, despite his relative youth, was selected to serve as *Mashpia* at one of the flourishing *Tom'chei T'mimim* yeshivos in Europe. He alone knew how little he desired such a position requiring such great responsibility. In *avoda* particularly, he regarded himself as deficient to the point that he was horrified at the very idea of becoming an educator and guide of an upcoming generation of *T'mimim*. Yet when he received the Rebbe's affirmative answer and blessing, he accepted immediately without hesitation. His acceptance of the Rebbe's higher authority was utterly spontaneous and devoid of self-interest.

He may not have reached Bentzion's fame or attracted massive crowds. He did not travel from one land to another or write articles in North America's most popular Jewish periodicals. His activities were internal and not so noticeable to the wider public. But within just a few years, he became widely recognized as a new force in Chassidic education and guidance. His students and alumni were immediately recognizable for their seriousness, high character and devotion to fulfilling whatever was expected of them.

As for Aharon, no one was surprised. Even while still in yeshiva, his fellow students had predicted his future role as a *Rosh Yeshiva*. Whenever other students had wanted to understand any subject fully, they knew Aharon was the one to approach. He had a unique talent to recognize immediately which points were likely unclear to his questioners and in a few moments to unravel whatever they did not understand. After entering *Tom'chei T'mimim*, he strongly emphasized avoiding shallow *pilpulim* and poorly based explanations, investing all his energy in direct, clear understanding of every concept. He quickly grew on the correct path of Torah study, which gave his learning a powerful momentum.

After just a few years in *kollel*, Aharon was offered a position as Talmud lecturer at one of the largest *Tom'chei T'mimim* yeshivos. Before long he advanced from lecturer of the lowest class to one of the highest. And when the elderly *Rosh Yeshiva* retired, Aharon was the natural choice to succeed him.

No one remembered exactly how their conversation opened. Aharon, Bentzion and Elimelech sat together at a truly brotherly *farbrengen*, surrounded by dozens of yeshiva students and young married men. A *farbrengen* of three such prominent Chassidim was no small event. The inspiring atmosphere of the days leading up to the major occasion helped to create the perfect setting, and the three *farbreng*ed for hours.

Bentzion told stories of how the Rebbe had helped in a miraculous way and other stories of Divine providence, all of which he had experienced firsthand. He clearly explained the lessons everyone could learn from each story. Elimelech emphasized the unique path of *avodas Hashem* revealed by the Rebbe. Aharon, as expected, explained and tried to illustrate how, without a fundamental grasp of *Nigleh*, it is impossible to understand *Chassidus* properly or to be a true *Chassid*. He also discussed the Rebbe's special approach to study of *Nigleh*.

As the night wore on and everyone became inspired by the *farbrengen*, the general mood was warm and open. The three started to relate their memories of the days when they began their journey to *Chassidus*.

Everyone smiled when Bentzion reminded Elimelech of their conversation about the Rebbe in those early days. Clapping Elimelech on the shoulder, he reminded him of a discussion they once had. "We were talking about the Rebbe and you tried to explain what a Rebbe is. You said the Rebbe is the head of the Jewish people and his function is like that of the head in the body, giving life to all the body's limbs. To illustrate your point, you told me that, at those very moments, the Rebbe was aware of what we were talking. Looking at you, I saw you were saying that with full sincerity, without even thinking that what you said might be considered unusual. At that moment I thought to myself that, come what may, that's something I'll never believe!"

Aharon and Elimelech burst out laughing at all their primitive ideas of those days. Aharon continued by sharing some of his own experiences:

"Our main problem back then was not that we did not understand what a Rebbe is. It was that we didn't understand spirituality at all, nor what a truly high level is. When I originally studied *Tanya*'s first twelve chapters, where the Alter Rebbe explains, among many other points, the various levels of *tzaddik v'tov lo* (usually understood to mean a *tzaddik* who doesn't suffer), *tzaddik v'ra lo* (a *tzaddik* who suffers), *rasha v'tov lo* (wicked man who doesn't suffer), *rasha v'ra lo* (a wicked man who suffers), and *beinoni* (the intermediate level between *tzaddik* and *rasha*), I couldn't digest the way he explained it.

"Suddenly I realized that the highest level of spiritual development I had ever conceived of was that of the *rasha v'tov lo* at his highest level. Because, after all, what was the greatest thing we could imagine? It was someone studying Torah all day, who is careful to fulfill all *mitzvos* in the best way, who knows of nothing but Torah and holiness. Now it turned out that such a Jew is a *rasha v'tov lo* in his highest state. So why's he called a *rasha*? Because he's capable of committing a sin, even if only once! So sin is not fully out of the question for him. Could we possibly imagine a Jew who would never commit even some slight sin? Doesn't Scripture tell us that 'There is no righteous person in the world who does [only] good and never sins.' Yet *Tanya* declares him to be a *rasha*, and proves that from the words of our Sages! So the highest level of which we could conceive was actually no more than a *rasha v'tov lo*.

"But then we learned there's an even higher level – a *beinoni*.

He's a Jew who never stops saying words of Torah, who never commits any sin, even in fulfilling the slightest directive of our Sages, and doesn't even have the sin of having an opportunity to reprove others for sinning but fails to do so!

"But if he's called a *beinoni* – the "intermediate" level – there must be someone even greater, a *tzaddik*. Given *Tanya*'s exalted description of a *beinoni*, who could possibly be even greater? For a long while I walked around with this question hammering away in my mind. Finally, we reached Chapter 10, which discusses the difference between a *beinoni* and a *tzaddik*. A *beinoni* needs to fight with his *yetzer hara* which tempts him to sin, but a *tzaddik* doesn't need to struggle at all, because he's never tempted by thoughts of sin. Within this category are two levels: *tzaddik v'ra lo* and *tzaddik v'tov lo*. The first does still have a minute degree of evil within him, but it's so negligible that it doesn't influence him in the slightest, while the second has no *yetzer hara* at all because he has transformed it into good.

"Can you possibly grasp what a revolution these chapters wrought in me? But that wasn't all. When I finally understood this subject of *rasha*, *beinoni*, and *tzaddik*, I came to a clear conclusion that although all these personalities might exist in theory, it's doubtful there's anyone in our generation who's actually a *beinoni*. As for *tzaddikim*, especially a *tzaddik v'tov lo*, there certainly couldn't be any in these lowly generations.

"After a while, I began to hear about the Rebbe. I decided that maybe, despite everything, a *tzaddik* really does live in our times, the Rebbe. Just then, when I had come to that conclusion, I happened to share this thought of mine with another student in *Tom'chei T'mimim*. But he burst out laughing.

"'Why are you laughing?' I asked."

"'I'm laughing at your limited conceptions,' he said. 'A Rebbe is way higher than a *tzaddik v'tov lo*. A Rebbe is a *neshoma k'lollis* – an inclusive soul, the head of all the Jewish people, as described in Chapter 2 of *Tanya*.'

"When I heard his words," Aharon continued, "I thought, either everyone is out of their mind or I'm the one who is totally clueless..."

Compassionate smiles spread across the faces of everyone listening. Some even looked at each other with astonishment, as if to say: Could it really be true that those who don't learn *Chassidus* really have such limited conceptions?

Aharon and Bentzion continued to describe their limited levels of understanding in those days. Meanwhile, Elimelech was sitting and listening. Everyone realized he wanted to share something, but was waiting for the right moment.

Dawn was already breaking and members of the first early morning *minyan* for *Shacharis* were already entering the *shul* and starting their preparations for prayer. It was then that Elimelech's quiet voice was heard, full of truth and *avoda*:

"Among those who haven't yet learned *Chassidus* are some who are blessed with pure souls and have heard a word or two here or there and know some of the true concepts about Torah, *Hashem*, and spirituality. But I would call their understanding a 'spiritual grasp,' while the understanding that *Chassidus* provides is a 'physical grasp.' On the surface, this definition may sound surprising, but I'll explain what I mean.

"That Jew who hasn't learned *Chassidus* might be aware that every Jew has a Divine soul, that every *mitzva* affects the higher spiritual worlds and also his soul and the world around him, and that every letter of the Torah expresses the Divine wisdom. But he understands all that in a spiritual way. In other words, he says the words, yet tries with all his might **not** to understand, because it's spirituality, and spirituality is distant from him; it's something he can't relate to or understand at all. Deliberately he strips these concepts of any connection with his understanding, elevating them beyond any possibility of discussion or trying to draw from them practical conclusions.

"*Chassidus*, on the other hand, teaches us to relate to these concepts with human logic, which can be termed (obviously within well-defined, clear limitations) 'physical.' When *Chassidus* tells us every Jew has a Divine soul, it's as if it has told us everyone has a heart and lungs. Just as the heart and lungs are clearly existent entities, likewise within every Jew exists a soul which is 'part of *Hashem* from Above, literally.' One who studies *Chassidus* relates to the fact of the soul's existence with the same degree of certainty as he does to his heart's existence. This lets him understand that the same Divine soul exists even within a Jew who vehemently fights against everything to do with *Yiddishkeit*. He views such a Jew like someone fighting all his life to prove there's no need for a heart and that a heart is superfluous; does that claim prove he has no heart?

"When *Chassidus* teaches that every *mitzva* fulfilled has an effect, the *Chassid* knows that effect to be true and real, in the same way that a nail is banged into a wall. He doesn't turn it into a spiritual concept. If we say that the very fulfillment of a *mitzva* has an effect, it means that donning physical *tefilin* on one's head, or that of any Jew, causes fear and terror to fall on the enemies of the Jewish people, as our Sages tell us, or that eating *matza* at the *Pesach seder* reinforces one's faith, as the *Zohar* tells us, as much as eating bread strengthens the body.

"This realism is the inheritance only of those who learn *Chassidus*. It's difficult to find anyone who doesn't learn *Chassidus* who is capable of relating this way to spiritual concepts. Interestingly, the same is true at the other extreme: *Chassidus* removes the physicality of spiritual concepts, while others expend much effort on bringing spiritual and Divine concepts down to physical understanding. It seems to be self-contradictory, but if we reflect on it, we'll find that it's really the same idea."

The three continued to discuss the superior qualities of *Chassidus* and how it had transformed their lives. They seemed utterly unaware of everything around them. So captivated were they by the *farbrengen*'s atmosphere that they didn't notice the clock or the large crowd gathered around.

Eventually all three fell silent, each of them deep in thought. The sound of *Shacharis* prayers came from far off in the front of the *shul*, but in the corner where they *farbrenge*d, silence reigned. The yeshiva students and others gathered around were all deep in thought, reflecting on what they had heard, no one daring to make a sound in those emotionally charged moments.

Suddenly Elimelech recovered from his reverie, banged on the table and cried out a traditional Chassidic interpretation of a passage from our morning prayers:

"'*Ashreinu*, how fortunate are we, how good is our portion [*chelkeinu*]!' We are so fortunate to be Jews, whose soul is a part [*chelek*] of *Hashem*. 'How pleasant is our lot,' that we study Torah and observe the *mitzvos*. 'How beautiful is our inheritance,' that we are *Chassidim*.

"And then comes a second *Ashreinu*, a special one on its own, 'How fortunate are we that we rise early, and then repeat in the evening, declaring *Sh'ma Yisroel*' – how doubly fortunate are we to be Chabad *Chassidim*, who have such deep appreciation of the *avoda* of *Sh'ma* and all our morning prayers, and who finish off the day with reading *Sh'ma* again before going to sleep, when we make a *cheshbon hanefesh*, a spiritual reassessment of our entire day!"

With these words the *farbrengen* ended, as everyone joined in to sing the time-honored, poignant Chabad melody on those words of *Ashreinu*.

As everyone stood up, Aharon grasped his two friends' hands in his own and repeated Rav Yosef's famous words in the Talmud:

"'If not for this day [when we became the Jewish nation who received the Torah], I'd be like any other Yosef in the street.' If not for the light of *Chassidus* and the Rebbe's great light, where would we all be today?"